ANCIENT
PUEBLO PEOPLES

SMITHSONIAN
EXPLORING THE ANCIENT WORLD
JEREMY A. SABLOFF, Editor

ANCIENT PUEBLO PEOPLES

By LINDA S. CORDELL

St. Remy Press • Montreal

Smithsonian Books • Washington, D.C.

EXPLORING THE ANCIENT WORLD
was produced by
ST. REMY PRESS

Publisher	Kenneth Winchester
President	Pierre Léveillé
Managing Editor	Carolyn Jackson
Managing Art Director	Diane Denoncourt
Production Manager	Michelle Turbide
Administrator	Natalie Watanabe

Staff for *ANCIENT PUEBLO PEOPLES*

Editors	Michael Ballantyne
	Alfred LeMaitre
Art Director	Philippe Arnoldi
Picture Editor	Christopher Jackson
Researcher	Olga Dzatko
Assistant Editor	Jennifer Meltzer
Photo Researcher	Geneviève Monette
Designer	Sara Grynspan
Illustrators	Maryse Doray
	Maryo Proulx
Systems Coordinator	Jean-Luc Roy
Administrative Assistant	Dominique Gagné
Indexer	Christine Jacobs
Proofreader	Judy Yelon

THE SMITHSONIAN INSTITUTION

Secretary	Robert McC. Adams
Assistant Secretary for External Affairs	Thomas E. Lovejoy
Director, Smithsonian Institution Press	Felix C. Lowe

SMITHSONIAN BOOKS

Editor-in-Chief	Patricia Gallagher
Senior Editor	Alexis Doster III
Editors	Amy Donovan
	Joe Goodwin
Assistant Editors	Brian D. Kennedy
	Sonia Reece
Senior Picture Editor	Frances C. Rowsell
Picture Editors	Carrie F. Bruns
	R. Jenny Takacs
Picture Research	V. Susan Guardado
Production Editor	Patricia Upchurch
Business Manager	Stephen J. Bergstrom

Library of Congress Cataloging-in-Publication Data
Cordell, Linda S.
  Ancient Pueblo peoples / Linda S. Cordell
       p. cm. — (Exploring the ancient world)
  Includes bibliographical references and index.
  ISBN 0-89599-038-5
  1. Pueblo Indians—Antiquities. 2. Pueblo Indians—History.
  3. Southwest, New—Antiquities. I. Title.   II. Series.
  E99.P9C76   1994
  979.004974—dc20   94-2308
                                                     CIP

Manufactured and printed in Canada.
First Edition

10 9 8 7 6 5 4 3 2 1

FRONT COVER PHOTO: *Spruce Tree House, in Mesa Verde National Park, Colorado, was home to Anasazi people who farmed the mesa-tops in the area.*

BACK COVER PHOTO: *This tall, black-on-white pitcher from Chaco Canyon is a fine example of Classic Anasazi pottery.*

CONTENTS

EDITOR'S FOREWORD

From the awe-inspiring dwellings in the cliffs of Mesa Verde to the impressive ruins of Pueblo Bonito in desolate Chaco Canyon and the striking designs on the pottery bowls of the Mimbres region, the images of ancient Pueblo culture in the American Southwest have become some of the best known hallmarks of Native American achievements in pre-Columbian North America. Tourists increasingly flock to see the many famous archaeological sites in the Southwest, as well as to visit modern Pueblo towns such as Taos and Acoma to admire Pueblo architecture, dances, and crafts.

What are the links between the Pueblo peoples of today and the ancient ruins that dot the landscape of such states as New Mexico and Colorado? A plethora of archaeological research is shedding new light on this important question and providing a better understanding than ever before of the nature of prehistoric and historic Pueblo culture. Drawing on her own extensive research and the vast literature of southwestern archaeology, as well as the preliminary results of important ongoing research, Professor Linda S. Cordell offers the reader a clear picture of the cultural trajectory of the Pueblo people over the last two millennia. New views on the rise of agriculture and emergence of settled village life in the Mogollon region, the beginnings of Pueblo architecture, the nature of the Chaco Canyon florescence, cultural connections with Mesoamerica to the south, and the reasons for the large-scale population movements prior to the arrival of the Spanish are among the topics she discusses and analyzes.

Professor Cordell's approach is especially exciting because it shows what modern scientific research has revealed about the critical roles that both the physical and cultural environments of the Southwest played in the shaping of the Pueblo way of life. In particular, she appraises recent studies of the influence of changing climatic conditions on the course of Pueblo cultural development, on the one hand, and the cultural interactions among villages and towns all over the Southwest, on the other. From such an appraisal, Professor Cordell is able to assess the significance of a dynamic southwestern environment as one of the key factors in the shaping of Pueblo culture through both time and space.

Professor Cordell is an internationally renowned authority on the ancient Southwest. She has excavated widely in New Mexico and is highly regarded for her excellent field research, teaching, and writing. She is the author of a widely acclaimed text on southwestern archaeology, *Prehistory of the Southwest* (1984), and has published numerous scholarly works on the subject. She also is the author of *Tijeras Canyon: Analysis of the Past* (1980) and has co-edited several important volumes including *Chilies to Chocolate: Food the Americas Gave the World* (1992), *Dynamics of Southwest Prehistory* (1989), published by the Smithsonian Institution Press, and *The Versatility of Kinship* (1980). Professor Cordell received her doctorate from the University of California at Santa Barbara and is Director of the University of Colorado Museum in Boulder. She previously has held the Irvine Chair in the Department of Anthropology at the California Academy of Sciences and has been Professor of Anthropology and Chair of the Department of Anthropology at the University of New Mexico.

In the pages that follow, Professor Cordell shares some of her vast expertise on the Southwest, both past and present, and describes the cutting edge of current archaeological research in the area. Readers will see clearly how recent archaeological advances have provided new insights into the long, rich development of Pueblo culture and the continuities and discontinuities between the prehistoric past and the vibrant Pueblo culture of the modern age.

Jeremy A. Sabloff,
University of Pittsburgh

The village of Oraibi, shown here in an 1898 photograph, was once the largest of the Hopi villages. Founded in about A.D. 1200, it is one of in what is now the United States.

the oldest continuously inhabited communities

1

INTRODUCTION

In the late 15th and early 16th centuries, when Europeans first encountered the aboriginal inhabitants of the Americas, they met societies as diverse in language, culture, and political organization as their own. Some Native Americans were hunters and gatherers who, out of economic necessity, lived in small, mobile groups. Others had built and lived in cities that were grander than many of the capitals of Europe. In some of these places, the descendants of those original Native Americans have continued to live for some 10,000 years. Of all the regions of the contiguous United States, it is today the Southwest that holds the largest number of indigenous peoples who still occupy their original homelands, retaining their ancient customs, beliefs, languages, and traditions.

Some of the people of the Southwest descended from the first aboriginal inhabitants of these lands. Others are scions of later arrivals. The Pueblo people of New Mexico and Arizona, who live in distinctive, compact towns (which in Spanish are known as *pueblos*) of adobe or stone and who maintain much of their traditional culture, are progeny of the original Native American occupants. They have made their homes among the mountains, mesas, canyons, and valleys of the Southwest for at least 10,000 years. The focus of this book is on the history of the Pueblos over that immense length of time.

The impressive cliff dwellings of Mesa Verde in Colorado and Canyon de Chelly in Arizona, the stark towers of Utah's Hovenweep, and the elegant multistoried stone towns of New Mexico's Chaco Canyon are among the still-visible legacies of the Pueblo ancestors whose homeland was—and still is—a region of great natural diversity. Forested mountains, pinyon- and juniper-dotted mesas (tablelands), dark canyons, and expanses of open, low-lying basins characterize the land. Much of the mesa country exceeds 5000 feet (1524 meters) in elevation, while a few of the peaks in the mountain ranges of southern Colorado, northern New Mexico, and central Arizona reach heights of almost 12,000 feet (3600 meters) and are snowcapped year-round. Most mountains, however, have alpine meadow or forests at their highest points. The basin country, at elevations of about 3000 to 4500 feet (900 to 1400 meters), supports a sparse cover of desert grasses. No matter how diverse the land, there is one climatic feature that unites the entire region—aridity. Water is precious for all of the area's inhabitants.

Summers are generally dry and hot, with daytime temperatures commonly in the range of 80° to 90°F. (25 to 35°C.). In winter, the high mesas and mountains are bitterly cold, windy, and covered with snow. Yet it is the deep mountain snows of winter that will melt in spring, feeding the thirsty land and the region's great rivers: the Colorado, Rio Grande, and San Juan. Spring is a time of strong winds and little or no rain. The earth becomes parched and dust storms obscure the normally clear skies. As the earth heats again in summer, powerful thunderstorms form along the mountains and sweep across the mesas. The brief but torrential storms bring welcome moisture to the land, but they also strip thin soils from slopes and cause ephemeral streams to overflow.

Despite the arid climate, the unpredictability and scarcity of rainfall, and the brief growing seasons—especially at high elevations—the Pueblos have been farmers for more than 2000 years, growing native American crops: corn, squashes, and beans. Originally, the crops themselves were obtained from peoples farther south in Mesoamerica, where they had been domesticated from wild varieties. Over the centuries, the Pueblos developed ingenious techniques for growing these crops successfully outside their original climatic range.

For archaeologists, Pueblo culture is most clearly defined by its agricultural way of life, and by excellence in particular arts—especially pottery—that often accompany a sedentary farming economy. As well as an agricultural livelihood, the Pueblo people shared compact settlements consisting of arrangements of contiguous rectangular rooms of one or more stories constructed around open plaza spaces. They also shared beliefs and customs that indicate close interaction among their communities over many hundreds or a few thousand years.

Today, there are 19 Pueblo villages in New Mexico and 12 Hopi Pueblo villages in Arizona. The New Mexican Pueblos are arranged along the Rio Grande and its tributaries from Isleta, just south of Albuquerque, to Taos, 70 miles (112 kilometers) north of Santa Fe, with an extension west of Isleta composed of the Pueblos of Laguna, Acoma, and Zuni that carry Pueblo lands to the New Mexico-Arizona border. The Hopi Pueblos are clustered on and around the three small mesas that form the southern margin of the large Black Mesa of Arizona. Although all of the Pueblos display cultural similarities, indicating common origins and similar histories, they differ in language as well as in the details of social and political organization, and religion.

The New Mexican Pueblos speak five different languages that fall into three language groups. The largest group, named Tanoan, consists of the languages called Tiwa, Tewa, and Towa. The second group is Keresan with two dialect variants, Eastern and Western Keresan. The third group has only one member, the Zuni language. Except for one village, Hano, where Tewa is spoken, the Hopi of Arizona speak Hopi, a language unrelated either to Zuni or the Tanoan languages. Given the diversity in language and the fact that interaction among the villages is a very old feature of Pueblo life, the Pueblos have been multilingual, of necessity, throughout most of their history. Nevertheless, villages that share a single language have particularly close ties. In clusters of villages where the same tongue is spoken, other cultural traits are commonly shared, reflecting close historical relationships, and the people think of themselves as closely related.

All of the New Mexican Pueblos north of Santa Fe speak Tanoan languages. From north to south, the Pueblos of Taos and Picuris speak Tiwa, while those living in San Juan, Santa Clara, San Ildefonso, Pojoaque, Nambe, and Tesuque speak Tewa. Historian Joe Sando, who is from Jemez Pueblo, points out that the northernmost villages were strongly influenced by non-Pueblo tribes, particularly the Jicarilla Apache and various Plains Indian groups. The influence is observable in such features as the wearing of beaded moccasins and braids. Most Pueblo men wear their long hair tied back in one *chongo*. However, men from Taos and Picuris, especially, wear braids. Taos and Picuris and their Jicarilla Apache neighbors also run foot races on their annual feast days. All of the eight northern Pueblos perform what they call the

Comanche Dance—an adaptation of a Plains Indian war dance—as one of their social dances. In addition to those occasions when the northern Pueblo ventured onto the Plains for communal hunts of buffalo and antelope, there was a great deal of trade, some of it quite formalized, between the northern Pueblos and Plains Indians during the 17th and 18th centuries.

South of Santa Fe, the southern Rio Grande Pueblos of New Mexico include three Tanoan-language-speaking villages: Jemez, where Towa is spoken and Isleta and Sandia where the language is Tiwa. The Tiwa spoken at Isleta and Sandia is slightly different than that used at Taos and Picuris, but the two variants are close enough that understanding is unhindered. Although Jemez is the only village where Towa is spoken today, Towa was also the language of Pecos Pueblo, an important village on the eastern edge of Pueblo country. When Pecos Pueblo was abandoned in 1838, the remnant of its once numerous population went to Jemez where their linguistic relatives were living and where their descendants continue to reside today. The other Pueblo villages south of Santa Fe speak Keresan, except for Zuni, the westernmost New Mexican Pueblo, where the Zuni language is spoken. Minor dialectical differences separate the Western Keresan that is spoken at Laguna and Acoma from the Eastern Keresan of Cochiti, San Felipe, Santa Ana, Santo Domingo, and Zia.

Although nearly all of the New Mexican Pueblos are a single settlement, Laguna is made up of six small villages located on either side of the Rio San Jose: Old Laguna, New Laguna, Seama, Encinal, Paguate, and Mesita. Today the Acoma occupy their ancestral village on a mesa top above the Rio San Jose and Acoma Creek, in addition to two newer villages, Acomita and McCarty's, below and to the north of Acoma Mesa. Today, Zuni is spoken at only one village. At the time of the first European explorations into Pueblo country in the 16th century, the Zuni people occupied six villages. The move to one village called Halona, now Zuni, took place in 1692.

According to Joe Sando, the southern New Mexican Pueblos have had more interaction among themselves during the historic period than they have had with other Native American peoples. They keep up their own traditional dances and costumes without having borrowed dances from the Apache or Plains groups. Sando notes that European-American culture has had a major impact on the dances of the Western Keresan-speaking villages of Acoma and Laguna, perhaps because the Santa Fe Railroad was built through their lands. Many Acoma and Laguna worked for the railroad, accepting assignments in Gallup, New Mexico; Winslow, Arizona; and in Barstow and Richmond in California. Such distant employment meant that although people would come home for traditional feast days and dances, they could not be in their home villages for the long periods of preparation and practice that precede these occasions. Although traditional dances continue to be performed, uninfluenced by Plains dances, costumes are decorated with store-bought materials that can be assembled quickly, rather than with traditional gathered evergreens.

The arid Southwest is the heartland of the Pueblos. Archaeologists divide the prehistoric Pueblos into two main traditions: the Anasazi and the Mogollon. The modern descendants of these ancient cultures live in villages clustered in northeastern Arizona and north-central New Mexico.

The Hopi of Arizona occupy 12 villages on the three Hopi mesas, which are numbered from east to west. The communities of Walpi, Sichomovi, and Hano (also called Tewa Village) are on First Mesa, the easternmost Hopi mesa. The Second (middle) Mesa communities are Shongopavi, Shipaulovi, and Mishongnovi. The communities of Third (west) Mesa are Oraibi, Lower Moenkopi, Hotevilla, Kyakotsmovi (New Oraibi), Upper Moenkopi, and Bacabi. At all of these, except for Hano, the language spoken is Hopi. Hano, on First Mesa, was founded in the 17th century by Tanoan-speaking Pueblos from the Galisteo Basin south of Santa Fe and from the Rio Chama country northwest of Santa Fe.

The New Mexican Pueblos bore the brunt of early and continued contact with the Spaniards. The Spanish explorer and military commander Francisco Vásquez de Coronado visited Zuni and the Rio Grande Pueblos in 1540. The first Spanish Colonial capital in New Mexico was established at San Gabriel del Yunge immediately across the Rio Grande from San Juan Pueblo in 1598. In 1610, the capital moved to Santa Fe. Seventy years later, on August 10, 1680, the New Mexican Pueblos rose in revolt against the Spaniards. The attempt to convert the Pueblos to Christianity and the subsequent suppression of their religion were key factors in the revolt. Twenty-one friars and a large number of settlers were killed in the uprising, and the survivors fled south of modern-day El Paso. Despite several armed attempts, the Spaniards were kept out of New Mexico until 1692-1693. The Reconquest, under Diego de Vargas, newly appointed Spanish governor of the northern province, was difficult, and not complete until 1696.

By the time of the Reconquest, Spanish law had changed, making illegal some of the more detested repressive practices. The official attitude toward the Pueblos became more humane and, over the course of the 18th century, the Rio Grande Pueblos made a variety of accommodations to European culture. Despite the early encounters between members of Coronado's expedition and the Zuni and Hopi in 1540-1541 and the subsequent sporadic attempts at Christian conversion, neither the Zuni nor the Hopi were effectively brought into the mission system. Furthermore, the Hopi were so distant from the base of Spanish power in Santa Fe, that they remained largely outside the control of the Colonial government.

Many of the observable cultural differences between the Hopi particularly and the Rio Grande Pueblos can be traced to the amount of exposure to, and reconciliation with, the invading Europeans. For example, New Mexican Pueblos have incorporated Spanish loanwords into their day-to-day speech, although not into the more formal language they use in ceremonies. The Hopi, on the other hand, have not incorporated Spanish loanwords at all. The New Mexican Pueblos celebrate the feast days of their patron saints with traditional pre-European dances performed, in part, in honor of the saint. The Hopi adhere to their traditional ritual calendars or modify the dates of dances for

The Pueblo peoples have been successful farmers for centuries and grow many varieties of corn that they developed to thrive in different soils and climatic conditions. Maintaining variety in the corn ensures that some will always survive.

other reasons. They may hold religious dances on weekends, for example, so that more Hopi who are living outside the reservation can attend.

For many Pueblos, historians, and anthropologists, the Hopi represent a "purer" version of Pueblo traditional life. While this may be true for some aspects of Pueblo culture, none of the Pueblo communities have remained static for the last 400 years of interaction with outsiders of European descent. The various Pueblo peoples have reached different accommodations with the changing human and political landscape they inhabit. The late Edward Dozier, an anthropologist and Santa Clara Pueblo man, characterized the Rio Grande Pueblo relationship to Spanish culture as one of compartmentalization. The Rio Grande Pueblos adopt both traditional and European customs, but keep them strictly separate in their minds. Hopi scholar Hartman Lomawaima describes the accommodation the Hopi have made as one of "Hopification," which he defines as "the synthesizing process by which an idea or thing became imbued with Hopi values ... a process by which Hopi view, test, analyze, and make decisions about the actions or impositions of alien cultures or elements." Lomawaima makes the important point that Hopification is not restricted to the fairly recent encounter between the Hopi and European-American culture. Because the Hopi have interacted with other Native American societies for millennia, this process is extremely ancient, one that has allowed Hopi culture both to change and, at the same time, remain traditionally Hopi.

As a group, the Pueblos share a number of cultural elements or traits that distinguish them from other Native American peoples. Some relate to the kind of economy they have; others are better understood as the result of common Pueblo history. All of the Pueblos have been successful farmers for centuries. The agricultural technology they have in common includes tools and knowledge that enables them to grow their crops reliably and to survive in the arid Southwest. Pueblo corn, originally derived from Mesoamerica, has been selected and adapted to the cooler and drier conditions in the Southwest. The Pueblos raise several varieties of corn, some adapted to different soil and climate conditions. Corn is not only basic to the economy of all the Pueblos, it is also of tremendous symbolic importance. Corn and corn pollen are significant elements in ritual and prayer.

All the Pueblos share a traditional knowledge that includes detailed information about the soils, drainage conditions, and the climatic patterns of their lands. Because the timing of planting, cultivating, irrigating or hand-watering, and harvesting are critical to successful farming, all of the Pueblos maintain calendar systems with which they mark the solstices, equinoxes, and the phases of the moon. The passing of seasons is tracked in a general way by observing the migrations of birds, the changing temperature of the air, and the color of foliage in the mountains. Those with special training make far more accurate astronomical observations by observing the rising and setting of the sun in relation to known landmarks. In such a manner the ritual calendar can be regulated to specific astronomical events. The Pueblos are also knowledgeable about the wild plants and animals on their lands that, throughout the centuries, have been essential as supplemental and emergency foods and as medicines.

All of the Pueblos used the same kinds of tools for food preparation and storage—wooden digging sticks were the universal agricultural tool. In all Pueblo settlements dried corn was ground into meal using a *mano* (hand stone) and *metate* (flat grinding stone), and pottery—a hallmark of Pueblo culture for centuries—was fashioned into containers to store, cook, and serve food. For centuries, the traditional Pueblo household has consisted of contiguous rectangular rooms with some rooms serving as living areas and others for storage, but the configuration of dwellings has changed over the same period of time. In all Pueblo villages, however, there are special rooms, called *kivas*, that are used for religious rituals.

Concern about the dry climate and unpredictable rainfall led to the prominence of rain and fertility in traditional Pueblo religion. The similarity among the Pueblos in the expression of this concern can also be related to Pueblo history. The use of pipes (cloud blowers) and smoking in ritual contexts is one such feature. All of the Pueblos also have a variety of organizations that are concerned with rain and fertility, hunting, curing, and warfare. Membership in any one of these organizations implies a willingness to assume responsibilities within the community. Members are recruited in various ways. Among the Rio Grande Pueblos, the entire population of each village belongs to one of two groups in addition to whatever other organizations there are. These two

These 20th-century Pueblo women are demonstrating the grinding of dried maize kernels using stones known as manos (hand stones) and metates (flat stones) set in bins built into the floor. This effective method has been employed by the Pueblo people for centuries.

groups, referred to as moieties (from the French, *moitié*, meaning half), have both social and religious functions. In some villages, the governance of the village alternates during the year, with one moiety and its leadership taking major responsibility in winter, the other in summer. When some traditional dances are performed, the moieties dance alternately in the plaza. The moieties also compete in foot races. In other villages, clans—descent groups composed of people who are related through a common ancestor—play a more central role in the organization of religious and political life. Clans play a significant religious role and are responsible for safeguarding valuable esoteric information. They are particularly important among the Hopi, Zuni, and Keresan villages.

Some of the similarities and differences among the living Pueblos are the result of a very recent phenomenon, the contact and interaction with Western European culture. Prior to this contact, the Pueblo way of life was greatly affected by a variety of events and processes that occurred gradually over the millennia. The acceptance of the basic cultivated plant varieties from Mesoamerica, trade and interaction with other pre-Columbian societies of the Western Hemisphere, and natural events such as changes in rainfall patterns, all had diverse effects on local populations.

The cosmologies and traditional histories of all the Pueblos are similar. They share a belief in the emergence of humans from an ancient underworld, when humans did not resemble their modern counterparts but possessed some animal characteristics; they share a period of migrations and wandering until the central place of each village is located; and they have in common the incorporation of more than one people in each village. Pueblos also use a variety of symbols that are best understood in terms of their common history: the association of cardinal directions (the zenith and nadir), for example, with colors. Participation in the *katchina* ceremonies is also virtually a pan-Pueblo characteristic. Katchinas are beneficent, semidivine ancestral beings, associated with rain, who visit the villages through masked impersonators. The belief system and its expression are, like any religion, complex and defy explication in a few sentences. Of particular interest to the archaeologist are the very rich visual iconography and symbolism associated with the katchina belief system because some of the specific symbols are preserved in rock art, in paintings on ceramics, and in ancient wall-murals.

The detailed traditional history of the Pueblo people is maintained through religious narration, ritual, dance, and mime—writing is not used. This esoteric information is not generally shared with outsiders, nor do outsiders possess the cultural background to understand it. Pueblo religion is both philosophy and traditional history at the same time.

The goal of this book is to trace the development of the shared elements and the variations in Pueblo culture through archaeology, a tool that is used to study the ancient history of cultures, including our own. In the absence of a written record that might provide information about the symbolic, religious, and intellectual aspects of cultures, archaeologists usually define cultures on the basis of material remains—houses, ceremonial structures, stone and bone tools, ceramics, food remains, etc. It is probably only rarely that any archaeological culture corresponds directly to living descendant societies.

Archaeologists working in the Southwest have defined two great traditions that are ancestral to the modern Pueblo, reflecting continuity in material culture. It cannot be assumed that an archaeological tradition corresponds to a particular language group or to a political entity such as a "tribe." The two traditions considered ancestral to the modern Pueblos are the Anasazi, based in the Colorado Plateau country, and the Mogollon of central Arizona and New Mexico. The name Anasazi has come to mean "ancient people," although the word itself is Navajo for "enemy ancestors." It is unfortunate that a non-Pueblo word has come to stand for a tradition that is certainly ancestral Pueblo. The term was first applied to the ruins of Mesa Verde in southwestern Colorado by Richard Wetherill, a rancher and trader who was the first Anglo-American to explore the site—in the winter of 1888-1889—and who knew and had worked with the Navajo. The name was sanctioned, somewhat later, by A. V. Kidder, the acknowledged dean of southwestern archaeology, because he felt it was less cumbersome than a more technical name that was a composite of two previously named temporal divisions of the tradition. The awkward composite term, Basketmaker-Pueblo, might be likened to referring to historic inhabitants of New Mexico as the Colonial-Territorial people or to New Englanders as Colonial-Early Statehoods. The name Mogollon (pronounced Muggy-own) was taken from the Mogollon Mountains of the central Arizona-New Mexico border. The mountains in turn were named for an 18th-century Spanish Colonial governor of New Mexico.

Given that archaeological cultures are defined on the basis of material remains and that pottery and architecture are among the most obvious features preserved in the Southwest, it is not surprising that these two classes of artifacts are important components of the definition of the Anasazi and Mogollon traditions. The Anasazi tradition extended from northern Arizona and New Mexico into southwestern Colorado and southeastern Utah. At times, the Anasazi lived in settlements composed of loosely arranged separate houses. Early in their development, the norm in Anasazi housing was a semi-subterranean structure that archaeologists call a pithouse. However, the Anasazi were the first in the Southwest to adopt compact villages of contiguous, rectangular, surface rooms. Anasazi pottery was built up by hand coiling (the potter's wheel was unknown in all of the Americas before the European invasion) and was shaped and finished by scraping and smoothing the surfaces with such tools as pieces of gourd and smooth stones. Anasazi pottery generally was fired to a light gray or white core color. When painted, the surface colors were most often black on white produced by using black paint on a background of white-firing slip clays.

Southwestern archaeologists use distinctions in pottery and architecture to differentiate prehistoric traditions. Anasazi and Mogollon potters built up the walls of jars and bowls with coils of clay, and then scraped the coils smooth. Anasazi pottery has gray paste and the painting is typically black on white. The water jar (olla), shown below left, is a relatively late (circa A.D. 1200) example from the San Juan River area. Mogollon pottery has a natural red or brown paste color. Before A.D. 1000, Mogollon pottery was often highly polished, or else featured red painted designs on a brown background, as in the examples shown below right.

Many of the best-known and well-visited sites in the Southwest belong to the Anasazi tradition. The spectacular ruins of Chaco Canyon are Anasazi, as are the cliff dwellings of Canyon de Chelly and Mesa Verde. The New Mexico pueblos of Tyounyi and Puye and their associated cave ruins, carved out of the deposits of soft volcanic rock called Bandelier tuff, are also Anasazi. Though much of the northern portion of the Anasazi area was abandoned during the prehistoric period, there is no doubt among archaeologists or the Pueblo people that their descendants are among the modern Pueblos.

The Mogollon tradition occupied an extensive area along the Arizona-New Mexico border, south of Anasazi territory, and extending into adjacent Sonora and Chihuahua. Typical Mogollon settlements were composed of loosely arranged pithouses. Mogollon ceramics also were made by hand coiling and finished by scraping and polishing, but the paste color is red-brown to brown rather than gray. Surface colors were well-polished deep red or, if painted, red on brown. After A.D. 1000, two important changes occurred in portions of the Mogollon area: one was the development of compact villages of contiguous rectangular rooms, with room blocks massed around open plazas; the other, the decoration of ceramics with black paint on a white slip. Although their sites are not as well known to the public as are those of the Anasazi, one Mogollon group—called Mimbres for the river that runs through their heartland—is known worldwide for the beauty of the ceramics they made in the 11th century. Much of the Mogollon region was also abandoned in prehistoric times, and archaeologists believe the descendants of the Mogollon are incorporated among the modern Pueblos, partic-

University of Arizona archaeologist Emil W. Haury (1904-1992) was a major figure in Southwestern archaeology whose career spanned more than 60 years. He received numerous awards for his archaeological research, and served as president of both the Society for American Archaeology and the American Anthropological Association.

ularly the Western Pueblo villages of the Hopi and Zuni. Modern Pueblos consider themselves to be descendants of more than one people.

Obviously, there are strong resemblances between the Anasazi and Mogollon traditions, and after A.D. 1000 both traditions are clearly Pueblo. In defining them as separate traditions, archaeologists emphasize differences in the pace of change in the two regions and rather minor differences in material culture inventories. For example, after A.D. 500 the Anasazi and Mogollon pithouses differ in shape and architectural details. Pithouses were in use longer in the Mogollon area than in Anasazi country. The Mogollon seem to have depended equally on wild game and corn, whereas the Anasazi came to depend more on corn supplemented by game.

In August 1927, Alfred Kidder invited southwestern archaeologists to gather at his Pecos Pueblo field camp in order to compare notes and create a unified system of nomenclature for the prehistoric developments in the Southwest. Their work resulted in a chronological framework, called the Pecos Classification, that is still in use among archaeologists today. When it was devised, there were no techniques available to assign calendar dates to the events and periods that are defined. Subsequently, dates were assigned on the basis of dendrochronology (tree-ring dating), radiocarbon dating, ceramic seriations, and other techniques. The Pecos Classification, while still used throughout the Anasazi area, may not be as precise within localities as is possible and desirable. Largely for this reason, specialists may use local frameworks for particular areas of interest.

The Mogollon tradition was first defined, and named, by Emil W. Haury, a monumental figure in southwestern archaeology whose career spanned more than 60 years. Haury based his description on a chronological sequence developed in the Mimbres Valley of New Mexico. Given the enormous size of the region over which Mogollon remains are found, there is variability in the timing and distribution of traits used as the backbone for the framework. Again, most specialists work with sequences that are developed for specific localities. A sequence that is more generalized, and somewhat parallels the Pecos Classification, was devised by the archaeologist Steven A. LeBlanc and his colleagues in the late 1970s. This scheme is now used by a number of other workers in the field.

Finally, a scheme that was designed to encompass the entire Southwest was developed during an advanced seminar for scholars held at the School of American Research in Santa Fe in 1983. That framework brought together the very precise chronologies available for many areas and relatively new paleoenvironmental reconstructions. With these as essential background, the conference sought to characterize major trends that occurred across the Southwest. Although referred to in the literature, this scheme has not yet been widely adopted as workers continue to use the local schemes appropriate to their areas.

In investigating cultures where writing did exist, archaeologists can usually ascribe specific events to a particular year. Where there is no writing, the problem becomes more difficult. Southwestern archaeology, however, enjoys a particular advantage, though the region has no written records. Here, tree-ring dating offers the same precision. The astronomer A. E. Douglass, working at Lowell Observatory in Flagstaff in the 1920s, developed the science of dendrochronology as part of his program to understand relationships between sunspot activity and climate. The science depends on the fact that among certain drought-resistant species of trees, the width of the ring that is produced each year depends in large measure on the amount of moisture available for the tree. Over a series of years in which there is variability in moisture, a pattern of wide and narrow rings is produced. Charts that reproduce the pattern for a given species of tree in a given area can be extended back from living trees to the first years of growth of the oldest trees in the area. Fortunately, the Anasazi and Mogollon used wooden beams in building their pueblos and pithouses. Beams in Pecos Pueblo and other archaeological sites, inhabited from the time before the Spaniards entered the Southwest and well into the historic period, allow the pattern to be traced backward before written records for the area. As older and older archaeological sites are excavated, the chronology derived from the wooden beams can be extended farther back.

Today, the tree-ring record for most parts of the Anasazi and much of the Mogollon areas reaches back to A.D. 300. Newly excavated sites, if they contain building wood, may be fitted into the master chart for their area. Thanks entirely to this remarkable tool, archaeologists working in the

DENDROCHRONOLOGY

The Anasazi and Mogollon used wooden beams to build their pithouses and pueblos, thus allowing archaeologists many years later to date the sites with great accuracy. The width of annual rings in the wood used for construction (mostly pinyon and ponderosa pine) varies depending on the amount of moisture the tree receives. Within any locality, the variation in ring width produces a distinctive pattern. The illustration below shows how the width of the annual growth rings of a sample taken from a living tree (A) can be matched with a sample from an older tree (B) and with wood used in pueblo construction (C) to build up a chronology extending back to prehistoric times. The dependence of ring width on moisture allows reconstruction of past climate from the tree-ring record.

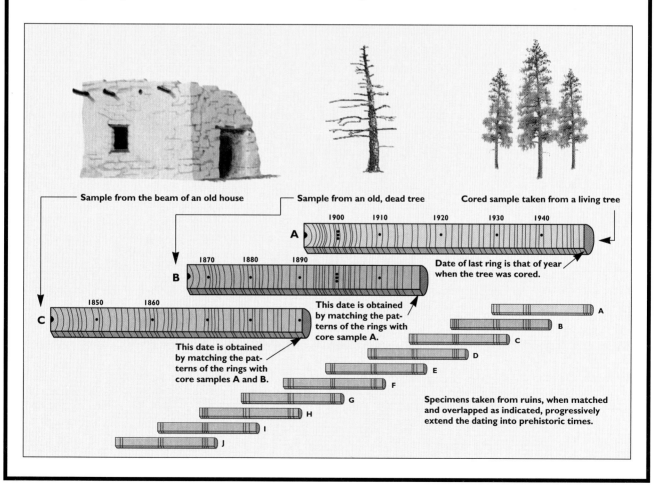

Sample from the beam of an old house

Sample from an old, dead tree

Cored sample taken from a living tree

A 1900 1910 1920 1930 1940

Date of last ring is that of year when the tree was cored.

B 1870 1880 1890

This date is obtained by matching the patterns of the rings with core sample A.

C 1850 1860

This date is obtained by matching the patterns of the rings with core samples A and B.

A
B
C
D
E
F
G
H
I
J

Specimens taken from ruins, when matched and overlapped as indicated, progressively extend the dating into prehistoric times.

Southwest can say, for example, that building activity at Mesa Verde ended before A.D. 1300, or that the Mogollon began to use black paint on white pottery around A.D. 1000, or that a large kiva was constructed at Tijeras Pueblo in A.D. 1313. Tree-ring dating also allows past climates to be studied in great detail because there are very precise models that describe the relationship between ring widths in appropriate tree species and the available moisture. For some parts of the Southwest, the amount of monthly precipitation has been traced back to A.D. 600.

Although dendrochronology is a wonderful tool, it cannot always be used. Many sites do not yield samples of wood, either because beams had already been removed in prehistoric times, probably to be used elsewhere, or because the wood had rotted. In certain places, the available wood used in buildings was not the kind that produces rings that vary predictably with moisture levels. Cottonwood and juniper, though plentiful in the region, are not useful for this reason. And in the few areas of the Southwest that are either very wet or very dry, the variability needed to produce readable patterns is missing. In all such situations—and they are many—the archaeologist must depend upon less-precise available tools, such as radiocarbon and archaeomagnetic dating, as well as the relative dating techniques that allow one to say that two events are contemporary or that one is older than the other. The most commonly used relative techniques are stratigraphy (the relative position of artifacts in the ground), and various kinds of orderings based on the types of ceramics produced.

This book divides the very long prehistoric sequence of the ancestral Pueblos into a few periods that are comparable to those used in the Pecos and general Mogollon classifications, but also extends those sequences both farther back and farther forward.

The kinds of information that can be brought to bear on the history of the Pueblos includes the traditional history of the people themselves; eyewitness accounts recorded by the Spanish explorers, officials, and colonists; descriptions of traditional Pueblo culture written by ethnographers, and interpretations made by archaeologists from ancient material remains. Each of these sources is influenced by cultural perspectives. Each one also pictures the world at slightly different scales, with different degrees of precision and resolution that are peculiar to their ways of understanding. The traditional perspective of the Pueblos includes, among other things, information about their origins and migrations. These are rich in metaphor, symbolism, and ethical and philosophical considerations, but may be less than specific when it comes to places and the timing and duration of events. It is the same for any traditional history, as either the life spans of people or the number of "begats" between events in the Old Testament demonstrates. Nevertheless, traditional Pueblo history is wonderfully informative regarding details of sites and artifacts that would otherwise be meaningless to archaeologists.

The first Europeans to enter the Southwest—some 40 years after the voyages of Columbus—were the Spaniards, whose empire had expanded west and north from their original power base in the Antilles. What they chose to record was conditioned by their past experiences and their expectations. They knew the impressive civilizations of central Mexico: the cities with royal and ceremonial precincts, wide avenues, pyramids, bustling markets, and crowded slums. These conquerors were compatriots and descendants of the people who had fought with Hernán Cortés at the time of the Aztec conquest in 1521 in what is now the Central Valley of Mexico. Yet official Spanish documents are silent about the daily life of the people they encountered. Modern scholars can be frustrated by the lack of common context for interpreting the chronicles. For example, disputes arise over locating places that are described in terms of the number of days' march from one camp to another. It is also baffling trying to understand why the Spaniards consistently used the term *estufa* (meaning oven) to refer to kivas. Still, when we acknowledge that 16th- and 17th-century Spanish culture is as foreign to today's American culture as either are to the ancient Pueblo culture, Spanish chronicle accounts can be very useful for their precision and for some of their detail.

Ethnographies written by trained anthropologists, and histories or travel accounts written by a variety of 19th-century American geographers, journalists, government agents, and others are exceptionally rich source materials used to flesh out the archaeological remains. These discussions do not apply to the entire time period for which there is an archaeological record. The truly ancient Southwest into which Native Americans ventured some 11,000 years ago has no analog in the writings of historians or ethnographers. When ethnographies and histories are used critically, they are invaluable references for a very broad range of interpretations.

The archaeological record is entirely a record of physical objects and their context. Without text, the individuals who produced the archaeological record are anonymous. The bones, the sherds, and the stone tools reveal a great deal about the most common activities of past lives and virtually nothing about the unique events or the words used to communicate about them. The artifactual record can sometimes be remarkably precise about dates, climate conditions, food sources, meals eaten, fuel burned, building materials used, sources of raw materials, and distances over which some items were exchanged. But the artifacts, house remains, and refuse will be mute about most kinds of social interactions, political groups, the specific meaning of symbols, and the motivations of the people who tended their crops, traded, prayed, fought, and loved.

Though this book is written from the point of view of archaeology, its frame of reference is enhanced by other perspectives: those of the modern Pueblos, the Spanish chroniclers, the historians, and the ethnographers who can give the ancient Pueblo people a voice.

The Grand Canyon marks the western frontier of ancient Pueblo culture. Between about A.D. 700 and 1100, Pueblo ancestors occupied both itself. Between A.D. 1150 and 1200, they abandoned the Grand Canyon completely.

2

THE DISTANT PAST: BEFORE THE PUEBLOS

canyon rims and fertile areas inside the canyon

As late as the 19th century, there still was considerable popular speculation about where Native Americans had come from—whether Europe or Asia or some mythical islands in between. Today, with the help of new data sources available to archaeology, we can link Native Americans ultimately to Asian ancestry. Physically, the Native American populations resemble Asian populations in outward appearance, in the distribution of blood group types, and in genetic composition as reflected by molecular data, such as DNA. Despite this consensus about the geographic origin of Native Americans, there is little agreement about the timing of their arrival in the New World. Information from three lines of evidence—bone form, molecular genetics, and linguistics—suggests that the Americas were peopled in three different migrations, each of which originated in Asia. The earliest brought people who were ancestral to most Native Americans, including the Pueblos. The second migration was of the ancestors of the Na-Dene peoples, a linguistic group who are today found throughout western Canada and Alaska, parts of the Pacific Northwest, northern California, and the Southwest, where they are represented by the several Apache tribes and the Navajo. The final migration from Asia, according to these sources, was of the Aleut and Inuit peoples (speakers of Aleut-Eskimo languages) of Alaska, Canada, and Greenland.

We know, since the discovery of certain crucial sites in New Mexico, that the Southwest was first inhabited more than 11,000 years ago, toward the end of the last glacial episode of the Pleistocene era. Archaeologists use the term PaleoIndian to refer to the people who lived in the Americas during this time. The term is meant to suggest an American equivalent to the Paleolithic of the Old World. Like the Old World's Paleolithic, the PaleoIndian period was a time before the development of agriculture, villages, and cities. In the Americas, however, there are no archaeological remains as ancient as those of the Old World's Lower and Middle Paleolithic—periods 3 million to 100,000 years ago that witnessed the evolution of *Homo sapiens.*

The later Pleistocene was a time of substantial fluctuation in climate, when the Southwest was both cooler and wetter than it is today. Large bodies of water covered places that are now dry basins. Lake Willard, for example, was one of five great Pleistocene lakes in the Estancia Basin of New Mexico. Other large lakes occurred in the vicinity of Lubbock, Texas, and in the plains of San Augustin, New Mexico. Reeds and willows grew thickly at the swampy margins of the lakes, trees extended farther down the slopes of mountains, and grasslands were abundant where today there is desert scrub. In addition to modern species, these Pleistocene landscapes supported a diverse animal life that included mammoths, camelids, giant sloths, and very large forms of bison, all now extinct.

Before the development of radiocarbon dating and other precise means of examining very ancient remains, the occurrence of stone tools and now-extinct Pleistocene fauna in the same deposits was crucial to demonstrating the very long period of time that Native Americans had been in the Western Hemisphere. In fact, the first conclusive evidence of the antiquity of Native Americans was uncovered at an archaeological site near the town of Folsom, New Mexico, in 1926 and 1927, when stone projectile points were found with the bones of an extinct form of Pleistocene bison. What became known as the Folsom site had been discovered several years earlier by George McJunkin, a self-educated, African-American cowboy and later ranch foreman, who had observed fossil bison bones eroding out of an arroyo after heavy rains. Later,

The dating of tools and projectile points excavated at Folsom, Clovis, and other sites in the Southwest has established that the ancestors of the Pueblo peoples first settled the region more than 11,000 years ago.

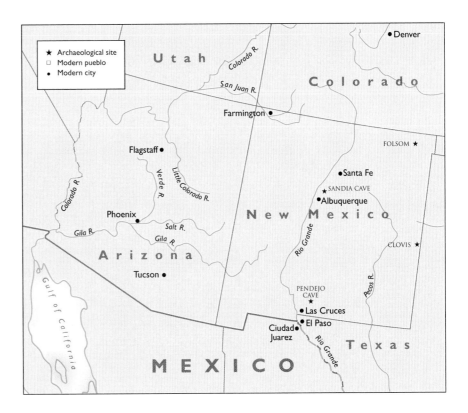

excavations at the site by paleontologists from the Colorado (now Denver) Museum of Natural History revealed beautifully crafted stone projectile points embedded in the bison bone. Although other stone points are now known to be older than Folsom, the Folsom points continue to be justifiably famous for their historical importance and for the skill with which they were made.

Over the years since the discovery of the Folsom site, a variety of PaleoIndian tool assemblages have been discovered and dated to the period between about 11,000 and 7000 years ago. The earliest of these is called Clovis, after the type site in southeastern New Mexico. Clovis artifacts are very widespread in North America. New methods of radiocarbon dating of the fossil, generally mammoth, bone found with Clovis points and recalibration of some key older dates, slightly revise the dating of Clovis to a tight cluster between 11,200 and 10,900 B.P. (Before Present is defined as being before 1950.) The question that is still most often debated is whether or not any cultural remains can be accepted as dating before Clovis.

The antiquity of Clovis, Folsom, and later PaleoIndian assemblages has been established by their association with specific fauna and by radiocarbon dating. There are about 70 sites, on both American continents, that have been proposed as possibly predating Clovis. As yet, these have not generally met the very exacting criteria archaeologists accept to establish antiquity in sites of reputedly late Pleistocene age. In the ancestral Pueblo homeland, two sites, both in New Mexico, are suggested to be older than Clovis—Sandia Cave in the Sandia Mountains just northeast of Albuquerque and Pendejo Cave near Orogrande, a town east of Las Cruces.

Sandia Cave was excavated in the 1930s, before radiocarbon dating had been invented. The distinguishing Sandia artifacts are single-shouldered projectile points, one type of which has had longitudinal flakes removed from the base on both faces, a technique called basal fluting. Fluting is characteristic of both Clovis and Folsom points. As well as these Sandia points, Sandia Cave also yielded Folsom points in different levels, mammoth and bison bones, mastodon teeth, and a claw core of a giant sloth. Years after their excavation, radiocarbon dates, ranging from 33,000 to 15,000 B.C. were obtained from some of the bone. The appropriateness of the dates has been questioned, however, because the association between the bone and the stone tools is uncertain. Although Sandia points have been found elsewhere on the surface of the ground, the only other excavated site yielding the type was a deflated dune site where Sandia and later materials were found mixed by geological processes. Some of the Sandia points have wear patterns on one lateral edge, which leads some archaeologists to suggest that the points may have been a specialized type of Clovis knife. Perhaps more important than the Sandia points themselves are scrapers, gouges, chisels, and other tools from Sandia levels in the cave that resemble stone tools from Pendejo Cave. The similarities between the two assemblages of tools support the interpretation that both are older than Clovis.

Excavations at Pendejo Cave near Orogrande were begun in 1990 in hopes that the site would yield perishable material dating to the time when corn was introduced into the Southwest. Excavation leader Richard S. MacNeish, whose work has been significant for documenting the domestication of corn in the Americas and broadening our understanding of PaleoIndian adaptations, noted that the upper levels of Pendejo Cave did yield perishable remains as expected, but as excavation continued a student worker "found the toe bone of an extinct horse in zone G. This changed everything; with this find we had entered the very controversial field of Early Man in the New World."

MacNeish believes that the most ancient materials from Pendejo Cave, called the Orogrande complex, may date to more than 40,000 years ago—in fact, he believes them to date to 55,000 years ago. Not as old as the Orogrande complex, but still considered older than Clovis, are the North Mesa and McGregor complexes that MacNeish dates between 40,000 and 13,000 years ago. The dates are based on stratigraphic position, association with extinct fauna, and many radiocarbon dates, only a few of which MacNeish deems improbable, and of which 28 are considered probably older than 12,900 B.P. Of particular interest is the fact that some of the North Mesa tools resemble those from the Sandia levels at Sandia Cave.

Many of the tools from the North Mesa and McGregor layers are flaked on one surface only, including projectile points that are like those MacNeish excavat-

Proof of the great antiquity of Native Americans was firmly established when spear points embedded between the ribs of an extinct form of bison were found. This stone spear point, bearing distinctive longitudinal grooves, or flutes, is one of several that were found with Pleistocene bison in a site near Folsom, New Mexico, in 1927. The find is a landmark in American archaeology.

30

ed at a deeply stratified cave in Peru called Ayacucho Rock Shelter, and that he named Ayacucho points. Other tool types from Pendejo include wedge choppers, burins (chisel-like tools), and scraping tools with working edges on one side or end. There are also bone tools and bones with flakes of flint tools embedded in them, including a prismatic flake at the "heel" end of a horse phalange. Preliminary reports of the work at Pendejo Cave are available, and both archaeologists and paleontologists have been able to visit the site. Nevertheless, many archaeologists view the very early dates—30,000 to 40,000 years Before Present—with skepticism, because none are derived from the artifacts themselves.

The well-documented PaleoIndian traditions of the Pueblo area are represented by the Clovis, Folsom, Plainview, Agate Basin, Firstview, and Cody tool complexes that also occur on the Great Plains. The tools that are characteristic of these traditions are types of stone projectile points that have been recovered from kill and butchering sites, especially of large game animals. The emphasis on hunting in these PaleoIndian economies is obvious because the sites and tools are often discovered when fossil bones erode out of the ground. In the drier, low-elevation western portion of the Southwest, some less specialized tool assemblages also date to the terminal Pleistocene. Tools from the lower levels of Ventana Cave, near Sells, Arizona, and those from the Sulphur Spring phase of the Cochise tradition found along Whitewater Creek, Arizona, are both probably as old as Clovis. Tools of the San Dieguito complex found at Ventana Cave and elsewhere in the western deserts, may be as old as Folsom.

Clovis assemblages are characterized by two types of fairly large—average length about 5.5 inches (14 centimeters)—bifacially flaked points with short single or multiple flutes. Fluting serves to thin the point in the region where it is hafted, without changing the width of the hafted portion. Fluting seems to be an American invention; it is unknown in Paleolithic sites of Europe or Asia. Other Clovis tools do have counterparts in the Old World, especially with tools found at sites in Eastern Europe and Western Siberia. The commonalities include the production of similar large blades, end scrapers, burins, bone tools that are called "shaft wrenches" or "bâtons de commandement," cylindrical bone points, unifacial flake tools, bone that has been flaked, the use of red ochre in burial contexts (admittedly very few PaleoIndian burials are known), and chopping of mammoth tusk around the circumference prior to snapping it in half.

The excavation of kill sites tends to skew our notions about Clovis and other PaleoIndians. Although the people who made Clovis tools butchered mammoth and used mammoth bone for tools, they also hunted bison and a great variety of smaller game. The distribution of Clovis sites in diverse environmental settings along with the presence of pounders and abrading tools suggests that the Clovis economy was one of hunting and gathering rather than one of highly specialized or nearly exclusive reliance on mammoth or other large Pleistocene game.

Folsom hunters pursued the large, Pleistocene species of bison in addition to smaller game such as antelope, canids (wolves and/or coyotes) and jackrabbits,

The fluted projectile point called the Clovis point is named after the New Mexico site where the first one was discovered in 1932. Generally made from fine-grained stone, such as obsidian, chert, or chalcedony, the points were 3 to 4 inches (7.5 to 10 centimeters) long, with fluting extending only partway up. When hafted to a wooden shaft, they made powerful hunting weapons. Clovis points are most often associated with remains of Pleistocene mammoth.

This distinctive wrench-like tool of mammoth bone was found at the Murray Springs, Arizona, Clovis site. Although it may have been used to straighten bone or wood spear shafts, similar artifacts recovered in European Upper Paleolithic sites are called "bâtons de commande-ment," a term that suggests they may have had a social rather than technologi-cal function.

after mammoth had become extinct. At Folsom kill sites, the number of bison taken averages about 16. This is small compared to later PaleoIndian times when the average number of bison per kill site is nearly 100. The change in number is a reflection of herd size, and that in turn is related to environmental conditions, rather than to development of more effective hunting skills after Folsom. Even later PaleoIndian kill sites were found to contain huge numbers of bison, the result of large herds being stampeded over cliffs. The stampede tactic only works, as archaeologist George C. Frison points out, when the herd is large enough, and the animals are trapped by those behind them so that they cannot retreat.

From the Folsom kill sites, the most distinctive artifact is the Folsom point, which is characterized by bifacial fluting for nearly the entire length of the point, and by very delicate bifacial, lateral flaking. Folsom points are smaller and thinner than Clovis points. They average about 2 to 3 inches (5 to 7 centimeters) in length. The way in which the long, longitudinal flutes were removed from Folsom points is not known, although several studies have successfully reproduced the points using different techniques, and at least two different step-by-step reconstructions have been developed based on finding the points that had been broken during manufacture. Because the number of points that had broken while they were being made is quite high (as much as 25 to 27 percent of the points), some archae-ologists have described the Folsom manufacturing process as wasteful. On the other hand, most archaeologists also consider Folsom points a mark of extraordi-nary ability and skill in stone working on the part of their makers.

Two carefully excavated Folsom camping sites provide detailed informa-tion about the range of Folsom tools and technology that is not available from kill locations. One of these is the Lindenmeier site, in northern Colorado, excavated in the 1930s by Frank H. H. Roberts, Jr., for the Smithsonian Institution. The other is the Hanson site, in northeastern Wyoming, excavated in 1975 by George Frison and reported in detail by Frison and Bruce A. Bradley.

The Hanson site was a camping location, probably not far from a bison kill. Analyses of bison bone found at the Hanson site indicate that nothing was wasted. Heavy hammer stones were used to break up long bones from which marrow was extracted. End scrapers were probably used to scrape hides, and as these are abundant in the assemblage, hide preparation was likely an important activity. Sharp cutting tools and eyed needles of bone that have been recovered from Folsom sites are evidence of an advanced technology of hide preparation. The hides themselves were probably used for clothing, lodge covers, and con-tainers. Woodworking was also considered to have been an important activity at the Hanson site, as reflected by choppers, coarse denticulates, and particular kinds of scrapers. Woodworking would have been important to the production of spears and throwing-sticks (called *atlatls*) if they were used. Again, one has the impression of highly competent hunter-gatherer societies living success-fully on the Plains and adjacent areas 10,000 years ago.

One of the very few Folsom camping sites (as opposed to bison-kill locations) to have been excavated is at Lindenmeier, northern Colorado. The site was excavated in 1930 by Frank H. H. Roberts, Jr., for the Smithsonian Institution. Although bones of Pleistocene bison feature prominently, the site also yielded remains of deer, elk, pronghorn antelope, fox, wolf, coyote, and rabbit. Lindenmeier seems to have been occupied periodically over several decades.

The Later PaleoIndian traditions are also known for their finely crafted spear and dart points, although fluting died out as a technique for thinning. The later points were thinned by bifacial, transverse parallel flaking or bifacial collateral flaking. The craftsmanship is remarkable. Other stone tools include various end and side scrapers, denticulates, notched flakes, and knives. The excavation of large, open kill sites rather than camping places or caves limits the amount that can be said about the diversity of artifacts used by PaleoIndians, especially about items made of perishable materials. In very rare instances, incised bone disks that may have been ornaments have been recovered from PaleoIndian sites, as has a unique collection of wooden spears. A small number of bone foreshafts, needles and beads, and flaking tools of antler tine have been excavated from PaleoIndian sites. But these are the only surviving artifacts of great antiquity. We have no examples of clothing, no hide containers to expand our knowledge of the PaleoIndian culture.

The PaleoIndian period was one during which climate fluctuated. There were episodes when it was cooler and wetter than it had been at other times. Yet, throughout the interval from 11,000 years ago until 9000 years ago, the overall climatic trend was toward reduced surface water, drier climate, and warmer summers. As the lakes and streams became smaller, grasslands expanded, providing habitat and especially forage for bison. Herd size seems to have increased after 9000 B.C., as reflected in the larger numbers of animals taken in kills. As conditions became even drier, the grasslands and bison retreated northward and the southwest slowly began to take on the characteristic climates and vegetation cover with which we are familiar today. Modern bison, much reduced in size from their Pleistocene counterparts, continued to graze along the eastern edge of what would become the Pueblo world. Elsewhere over much of the Colorado Plateau—the ancestral Pueblo homeland—elk and deer were the most abundant remaining large game. Rocky Mountain bighorn sheep and antelope were also present, but were smaller and fewer in number. Eventually, by about 8500 years ago, it became impossible to sustain a way of life focused primarily on hunting large game. A more generalized hunting and gathering way of life developed in the Southwest.

Throughout the world, the shift from Pleistocene to modern climates, vegetation patterns, and fauna necessitated changes in human economies. The changes resulted in somewhat reduced mobility and more dependence on locally available resources. The human adaptation to local resources was a

The vast tract of arid grassland extending from Alaska to the Gulf of Mexico was once known as the Great Bison Belt. Plains PaleoIndians hunted the bison by using a spear-thrower, called an atlatl, which enhanced the power of the throwing arm. This hunting technique is portrayed in a mural at the Denver Museum of Natural History.

worldwide phenomenon. Along coasts, major rivers and lakeshores, locally available resources included fish and shellfish. In forested areas, nuts, berries, deer, and other forest species became important foods. In the far north, big game hunting remained economically central, because the growing season precludes dependence on plant foods, but the game taken were modern forms. In semiarid regions, such as the Southwest, hunting several kinds of animals, gathering plant foods and preparing meal or flour from wild grass seeds characterized the period. In Europe and southwest Asia, the period is called the Mesolithic. Throughout the Americas, the term Archaic is used. The specific character of the adaptation depended, of course, on which local resources—fish, nuts, berries, game, or wild grasses—were available.

In the Southwest, the Archaic is dated from 8000 years ago to about 1800 or 2000 years ago. The ending date coincides with the appearance of ceramics and relatively substantial residential architecture that reflect a commitment to horticulture greater than that of the Archaic. Given this long period of time, it is not surprising that archaeologists customarily divide the Archaic into subperiods, generally referred to as Early, Middle, and Late. The Early Archaic dates from about 8000 to 6000 B.P.; the Middle Archaic from about 6000 to 4000 B.P., and the Late Archaic dates from about 4000 B.P. to about 1800 B.P. Paleoenvironmental reconstruction for the Colorado Plateau suggests that the pinyon-juniper woodland, which today is characteristic between about 5200 feet (1600 meters) and 6800 feet (2100 meters), was established by about 8000 years ago. With one major exception, climate during the Archaic as a whole is seen as slightly more moist and cool than it is today. The exception was first noted by

Beautifully crafted stone projectile points have been found at sites throughout the Southwest. These points are named according to the location in which they were found, as well as their stratigraphic position at that location. Sandia and Ventana points may be among the oldest known in the United States. Later PaleoIndian assemblages, such as Agate Basin and Cody, are known for fine craftsmanship, and were used on spears. The top row shows the transition from late Paleolithic to Archaic styles. Archaic points are more often made of local materials—although less finely—and reflect a more sedentary lifestyle, with a greater dependence on plant foods.

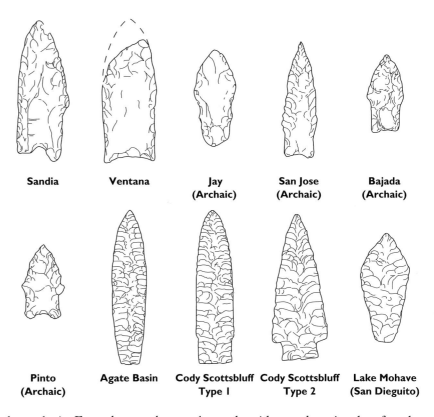

Sandia   **Ventana**   **Jay (Archaic)**   **San Jose (Archaic)**   **Bajada (Archaic)**

Pinto (Archaic)   **Agate Basin**   **Cody Scottsbluff Type 1**   **Cody Scottsbluff Type 2**   **Lake Mohave (San Dieguito)**

the geologist Ernst Antevs. Antevs observed a widespread erosional surface that he believed indicated a period during which it was both warmer and drier than it is today; accordingly, he named the interval the Altithermal. Both the timing and the nature of the Altithermal in Western North America have been debated for years. For the Colorado Plateau, evidence for the Altithermal is somewhat variable in nature. The importance of dating and understanding the Altithermal derives from the fact that a number of scholars believe that a warm and dry Altithermal may have stressed Archaic populations to the extent of encouraging major changes in their locations if not their economies.

PaleoIndian sites are relatively rare on the landscape because of their great age. When found, however, PaleoIndian sites are characterized by very specialized, distinctive weaponry and the very obvious large bones of Pleistocene game animals. By contrast, Archaic sites have a more generalized tool kit that includes stone tools for processing plant foods as well as weapons. Archaic tools are often made of locally available stone, usually of variable quality. When Archaic sites contain animal bones, these are of smaller, modern species. In the Southwest, these characteristics make Archaic sites less visible archaeologically than either the older PaleoIndian sites or the much more recent Pueblo sites with their pottery and architectural remains. In part for this reason, a great deal of Archaic archaeology had been somewhat neglected by archaeologists until recently. Today, the record of Archaic adaptations is quite good for some time periods and parts of the Southwest. For others, the data are still scant.

A major effort to chronicle both the cultural sequence and adaptations of the Archaic from the perspective of Pueblo ancestry was made by southwestern archaeologist Cynthia Irwin-Williams, who also had considerable experience with PaleoIndian sites. Irwin-Williams focused her research on a series of sites in the Arroyo Cuervo region, in the drainage of the Rio Puerco on the east just northwest of Albuquerque. The sites she excavated included cave or rock-shelter locations and open camping places that were found on eroded sand dunes. Beginning in the late 1960s, Irwin-Williams defined an Archaic tradition, which she named Oshara, that she believed represented an unbroken continuum from the beginning of the Archaic to the modern Pueblos. At the same time, she recognized that as a way of life, the Oshara tradition shared many characteristics with other Archaic manifestations in the western United States. She used the name *Picosa*, an acronym derived from the names of Archaic projectile point types, to refer to the way of life in general.

The diagnostic, or distinguishing, tools of the Early Archaic (8000 to 6000 B.P.) are dart or spear points. The particular types are Pinto Basin and San Jose points throughout much of the Southwest Basin and Range country and Jay and Bajada points in the Arroyo Cuervo area. These points differ from PaleoIndian points primarily by being notched rather than smoothly lanceolate in form. The notching suggests a change in hafting methods. Ground stone tools, such as small hand stones (called manos in the Southwest) and milling stones (called metates), are commonly part of the stone tool assemblage. Knives, scrapers, drills, and gravers also occur but do not vary much over time as do the projectile points.

The subsistence economy depended upon game such as elk, deer, antelope, and mountain sheep, but also included a diet of rabbit and even smaller animals such as pack rats and squirrels. Plant foods recognized in excavations are rice grass, goosefoot, dropseed, and prickly pear.

The small size and ephemeral nature of most Early Archaic sites suggest that local groups consisted of a few, highly mobile families. Archaeologists suggest that even some very large areas, such as Black Mesa, Arizona (some 485 square miles or 1256 square kilometers) may have been visited only occasionally, or perhaps periodically, by small groups during the entire 2000 years of the Early Archaic. Finally, although dating rock art is an exercise fraught with difficulty, some widespread abstract panels and elements, such as meanders, circles, and chain designs are thought to be of Early Archaic age. If so, the art may be the most durable and prominent evidence we have of the Early Archaic people.

If the Early Archaic is poorly understood because of a paucity of data, the Middle Archaic is both poorly known and controversial. Once again, projectile point types are the diagnostic chronological indicators. In the Arroyo Cuervo region, Irwin-Williams defined the San Jose phase that she considered spanned the period from about 5000 to 3800 B.P. San Jose points, which are similar to Bajada points, but are shorter, more often serrated, and have slightly expanded stems, are diagnostic tools of the period. The rest of the San Jose stone tool assemblage is dominated by rough scrapers and large, heavy chopping tools. Basin-shaped grinding slabs and small cobble manos are thought to indicate increased efficiency in the grinding of seeds. Another improvement is the large, cobble-filled, subsurface or surface ovens. Irwin-Williams interpreted the environment of the Middle Archaic in the Arroyo Cuervo as one of increased moisture. Although the mobile hunting and gathering way of life continued, she suggests that extensive refuse stains at some sites also suggest more intensive, probably repeated, occupation.

In contrast to this view from the Arroyo Cuervo, archaeologist R. G. Matson, in a recent compendium and review of the Southwest Archaic, argues that there is little evidence of any occupation at all on the Colorado Plateau itself. Some sites on the Plateau periphery, such as Cowboy Cave and Sudden Shelter, in southeastern Utah, manifest Early Archaic and Late Archaic occupations, but only sparse indications that they were used during the Middle Archaic. For example, excavations at Sudden Shelter yielded 298 projectile points from Early Archaic deposits and only 46 points for the Middle Archaic, despite approximately equal lengths of time for the two periods. Matson concludes that either the Colorado Plateau was deserted during the Middle Archaic or that there was such a drastic change in settlement patterns that certain locations that had been occupied during both earlier and later periods were not used at all. If this was the case, Matson suggests that sites used only during the Middle Archaic should be found in areas and settings outside the Plateau. Matson attributes the proposed dramatic change in settlement strategy to the effects of the Altithermal.

In fact, one of the areas that does show intensive occupation by foragers during the Middle Archaic (in addition to the Arroyo Cuervo where there is evidence, but not in great abundance) is the Mogollon highlands of the southern half of the New Mexico-Arizona border country. The kinds of projectile points associated with the Middle Archaic in the Mogollon highlands include points similar to San Jose and Pinto forms, with expanding indented bases, and those similar to Augustin and Gypsum Cave points, with contracting convex bases. The base forms suggest somewhat different methods of hafting. The Middle Archaic is well represented by sites in this region and dated sites of this time period indicate intensive use of valley and basin areas.

It is entirely possible that the Altithermal or something like it affected the central Colorado Plateau and the Mogollon highlands differently. One argument is that the Mogollon highlands may have been part of a larger "refuge area" for displaced foragers from the more northern settings. At present, despite a respectable number of excavated sites in both regions, neither the details of Middle Archaic climate or human population density are known with the kind of precision that is adequate for resolving contrasting models of this 2000-year-long, historically remote time.

It was during the later part of the Archaic, between about 4000 and 1800 years ago, that ancestral Pueblo people began cultivating corn. This event forever altered their way of life and set them apart from the peoples around them on the Great Plains and in the Great Basin who remained hunter-gatherers until historic times. The change from foraging to growing food was a necessary precondition for the development of villages and towns among the Anasazi and Mogollon. Corn was essential to the 2000 years of the evolution of Pueblo society.

The period of time in the Pueblo homeland after the people began growing corn but before they began using pottery is referred to as Basketmaker II or the Late Archaic, depending upon whether one is speaking of the Anasazi or Mogollon areas. At the time that the term Basketmaker was adopted by southwestern archaeologists in 1927, there was little or no evidence of the Archaic. Knowing that a period during which the Anasazi were foragers without corn must have existed, what we now call the Archaic was named Basketmaker I and at the time it was a hypothetical stage. The beginning of recognizable Anasazi life, with agriculture, basketry, and stone tools, was thus Basketmaker II. The term was used as early as 1894 by B. T. B. Hyde, and probably by the Wetherill brothers whom Hyde financed through the American Museum of Natural History. The Wetherill brothers (Richard, Al, John, Clayton, and Win) were the first European-Americans to see and explore the ruins of Mesa Verde, and they brought their experience to the attention of the scientific community and the public. With Hyde's backing, the Wetherills also explored the cliffs and rock shelters of the Grand Gulch region of southeastern Utah which yielded an abundance of Basketmaker remains. By the 1890s, it was generally understood that the Basketmakers were different from and older than the later Pueblos.

Basketmaker culture was much like its predecessors, as described above. Basketmaker peoples lived mobile lives as foragers who also cultivated corn. They used spears with stone tips and spear throwers. They ground wild seeds and corn with small manos and metates. Community size continued to be small and there was little investment in housing. Basketmaker II houses have been excavated along the northern San Juan River in both Colorado and New Mexico. These houses are small (some 15 feet or 4.5 meters in diameter), circular structures with slightly depressed, saucer-shaped floors, cribbed log walls, and roofs that were plastered with mud. Storage cists were much like the houses except that they were even smaller and were often lined with upright stone slabs.

Unlike their ancestors, Basketmaker II people used rock shelters to store their supplies of food and equipment and to bury some of their dead. The naturally dry caves desiccated and preserved the bodies and otherwise perishable goods, so that from these sites archaeologists have a remarkable record of the people themselves and the items they used in daily life and placed with the dead. It would surely be wrong to think of the Basketmaker rock shelters as typical of all Basketmaker sites or the artifacts as representing the full range of types of objects the Basketmakers made and used. Yet to diminish the importance of the burial caves as possibly atypical would deprive us of an incredible glimpse of these ancient people.

By far the richest and most famous Basketmaker II site is White Dog Cave in northeastern Arizona, excavated in 1915 by Alfred V. Kidder and Samuel J. Guernsey for the Peabody Museum of Harvard. The cave's name derives from one of the excavated dog burials. A long-haired white dog with brown spots, about the size of a small collie, was buried with an adult male, who may have been the dog's owner. The white dog represents one type or breed of ancient Pueblo dog. The other, also first known from White Dog Cave, is a small terrier-like dog with short hair, in this case white with black spots.

The men and women buried in White Dog Cave were rather small in stature; men typically about 5 feet (1.5 meters) tall, women somewhat shorter. They looked like modern Native Americans, with straight, black, somewhat coarse hair, and medium to light brown skin color. Babies had lighter skin and finer hair. The women's hair was cut, rather unevenly, presumably having served as a supply of fiber for woven fabric. Both human and dog hair was used in Basketmaker weaving. The men wore their hair long, tied in three bunches—one on each side of the head and one in the back. Some, but not all of the men, also had a queue made of hair taken from the crown of their heads.

Women who were buried in White Dog Cave wore necklaces of beads made of stone, snail shell, abalone shell, or seeds; but none of turquoise, a stone later very important to the Anasazi. Elsewhere on the Colorado Plateau, particularly in and around Canyon de Chelly, some Basketmaker II burials were richly adorned with turquoise ornaments, shell, and stone beads. In these western Anasazi areas, the Basketmaker II burials have more elaborate jewelry than do later burials from the same places. This is a finding that is surprising because luxury items and jewelry are more often associated with advanced societies dependent on agriculture, not with mobile foragers who depended minimally on crops.

Women also wore an apron of soft, loose-hanging fibers about a foot long and bound to a waist cord of the same material. Men were buried without even this scanty clothing. Both sexes, however, wore—and were buried with—woven, square-toed sandals. Frequently a new pair was interred with the body. These were made of yucca fiber or yucca and apocynum (Indian hemp). The open sandal was held in place by one toe loop and a heel loop, with a tie passing from loop to loop around the ankle. One large type of sandal seems to have been used as an overshoe, since they are often found covered with mud.

In addition to carrying and storage, Basketmakers used their handwoven baskets as cache liners to protect grain and other food items being stored in underground cists. The basket was inverted and placed over the produce and held secure with a covering slab of stone. This fine example, measuring 25 inches (63.5 centimeters) at its open end, was found at Glen Canyon, Utah.

39

Both sexes also used robes for warmth. One kind of robe was made of tanned deerskin, sometimes with leather tie straps attached to hold it closed across the chest. The other type was a light, warm covering made by wrapping strips of rabbit fur around yucca cords that were then tied together in close parallel rows. Babies had soft blankets made from the bellies of rabbit skins and diapers made from the soft interior bark of juniper. They had portable carrying cradles made of straight rods tied in a neat cross to a stick bent into an oval form.

In addition to the fabric made for clothing, the dry Basketmaker caves preserve various handwoven items of daily use, all of which are a tribute to the skill of these people. Slip-noose snares made of fine string, usually human hair, could be used for taking small game and birds. Larger nets were made to stretch across the mouth of a gully or arroyo and block all game driven toward it by groups of people. White Dog Cave yielded a net that is 240 feet (73.1 meters) long and over 3 feet (1 meter) in width, with a 2.5-inch (6.35 centimeters) mesh of fine fiber string, composed of nearly 4 miles (6.4 kilometers) of cordage. Dark and lighter-color fibers were woven into the net in a pattern designed to encourage the trapped animals to see the dark areas as potential escape holes and run toward them, thus trapping themselves in the net where they could be quickly killed.

Large, conical, burden baskets and tumplines were also handwoven, as were trays used for winnowing and also for parching seeds. One unusually shaped type of burden basket was lined with pitch and used to carry water. Smaller baskets were commonly used for storage, and have been found filled with wild seeds, corn kernels, and weaving materials.

Although most foods were probably roasted or baked, some tightly woven baskets were apparently used to boil meat and stews. Using sticks for tongs, the Basketmakers placed heated rocks in the liquid in the basket, replacing them with hot stones as they cooled, until the food was done. The Basketmakers also made twined, seamless, soft bags of an oval shape. These were made of fine yucca and/or apocynum fiber. When they buried their dead, the Basketmakers often used a soft bag, sometimes split on one side, as a shroud for the flexed body. A large basket might also be inverted over the head of the deceased.

Bags and baskets were decorated with woven or painted designs in earthen colors; red from iron-oxide powder, yellow from limonite (yellow ochre), white from white clay, each mixed with water or grease. Brown, black, and blue pigments were obtained from plants and also mixed with water or grease. These colors were also used to paint figures on the rock walls of cliff faces near their caves. The typical Basketmaker human figure has broad shoulders and a blocky body with stick-like arms and legs. Another motif common to Basketmaker caves is their hand prints, also left in pigment.

Archaeologist Charles Avery Amsden worked for many years among the caves and ruins of the Colorado Plateau. Amsden wrote *Prehistoric Southwesterners From Basketmaker to Pueblo*, one of the finest and most accessible works about the Basketmakers for the general public. In the book, he wrote:

> It [archaeology] tells much of the life of the body and the work of the hands, little of the life of the spirit and the work of the mind. Like a painting, it can give us no more than the eye can see and the imagination conjure from its revelations. We must suppose that the Basketmakers were as active in mind as they obviously were in body, with a wealth of legend, poetry, ceremonial, social usage, and organization, that we can never hope to recapture except vicariously, through their modern kindred and heritors.

A glimpse into what may be the darker side of Basketmaker spiritualism is revealed in some of their burials. A fairly frequent pattern is the removal of heads and long bones from the grave after burial and attempts to protect the head through concealment. In one instance, the body of a young woman had been buried at White Dog Cave, accompanied by a trophy scalp made of skin from a human head. In the Basketmaker II caves, the remains of fire are often found associated with burials and some human bones are burned. It is very difficult to understand the set of beliefs that formed the context for these strange treatments of human remains, except by suggesting ideas associated with witchcraft or fear of sorcery. The precise nature of the beliefs is part of the life of the mind that, as Amsden indicates, is difficult for archaeology to reconstruct. Yet, as with much of Basketmaker culture, these unusual aspects of mortuary behavior have continuities and parallels in later Anasazi times.

Archaeologists see the Mogollon Late Archaic and Anasazi Basketmaker II as a time when patterns were established that survive into later portions of the Mogollon and Anasazi traditions. The continuities include planting corn and squash, perhaps with considerable dependence on these crops; hunting and gathering; production of textiles, especially sandals and baskets; the use of grinding stones; the use of small circular dwellings and of storage pits; making jewelry of marine shell, turquoise, other stones and seeds; painting on suitable rock surfaces; and burials that suggest belief in and fear of witchcraft and sorcery. Agriculture may have played a major role in encouraging or permitting these developments. Certainly, agriculture became the linchpin for much of ancient Pueblo life.

By about 1500 B.C., a strain of corn that originated in Mexico had appeared in what was to become the American Southwest. The addition
be stored for many months changed both the diet and the entire way of life of the Pueblo people. Corn is still the main food crop grown by

3

AGRICULTURE: THE BASIS OF PUEBLO LIFE

The Pueblo people have been successful farmers for more than 2000 years. Maize (*Zea mays*)—what we call corn—is the grain crop that has long been the foundation of Pueblo economy and was the key food plant grown by Pueblo ancestors. From the archaeological record we know that corn and squash were the first domestic crops adopted into the Southwest, and that beans were added only slightly later. We also know that these crops were first domesticated far to the south in what is now Mexico,

of a food with high nutritional value that could Pueblo farmers.

though we cannot know the precise way in which they were obtained, whether through trade, ritualized exchanges, or more casual interactions among groups of people.

The southwesterners who accepted corn and squash were Late Archaic foragers. Eventually, corn, beans, and squash were planted throughout the ancient Pueblo world, and served as the basis of village life. Later in Southwest prehistory, after people had made an economic commitment to farming and had come to settle down in hamlets, additional crops were accepted from Mesoamerica and incorporated into the Pueblo resource base. These crops included cotton, green-striped cushaw squash, and sieva beans. Cotton was grown widely throughout Pueblo country in locations where the growing season is adequately long, and its fibers used to produce textiles. However, cotton seeds are also edible and the crop may have been accepted in part as a food. Finally, a domestic pigweed (*Amaranthus hypochondriacus*) was grown late in prehistoric times in some parts of Pueblo country. This plant was (and still is) widely cultivated in Mexico. The ancestor of the domestic form is a native plant in Arizona, and it is possible that its cousin was domesticated in the Southwest.

Research by botanists and archaeologists has long been concerned with documenting the history of the domestication and diversification of corn. Within the past decade or so, archaeologists especially have become interested in better understanding the cultural context into which corn was accepted. The first corn grown in the Southwest probably required a great deal of work to cultivate and was not highly productive. It is therefore critical to understand why it was adopted. One current suggestion is that at first corn was a supplemental crop that could be stored, and that it was most useful among people whose mobility and access to wild resources had been restricted.

Archaeologists have long been curious about when and how corn was transferred from its original home in tropical Mesoamerica to the Southwest. As part of this interest, a series of cave and rock-shelter sites was excavated in the hope that within their protective walls, they would contain the otherwise perishable remnants of corn. Archaeologists wanted to find the earliest types of corn brought to the Southwest, and to do so they needed the right supporting evidence. They needed to find corn in a context that had no pottery remains—indicating an early, pre-pottery age for the corn—and they needed to find the types of corn botanists considered primitive. In 1948, an expedition from Harvard University, led by Herbert W. Dick, who was then an advanced graduate student, found precisely such evidence at Bat Cave in central New Mexico.

Bat Cave is a dark, impressive, high-ceiling rock shelter in a massive volcanic ridge. The cave overlooks the San Augustin Plain, a remnant of a large Pleistocene lake. The cave and small side fissures, about 130 feet (40 meters) above the plain, were formed by erosion of the volcanic conglomerate rock by

Excavations at Bat Cave, in the uplands of west-central New Mexico, have provided important clues as to when corn was introduced into the Pueblo region. Following initial excavations during the 1940s, corn kernels found in the cave were thought to date to 4000 to 2500 B.C. However, radiocarbon dating carried out on samples excavated in the 1980s now suggests that corn was introduced around 1450 B.C.

wave action on the ancient lake. Today, fossil beach ridges are clearly visible along the margins of the plain. Bison and antelope grazed on the fertile plain below well into the historic period. At an elevation of just over 6500 feet (2000 meters), the cave is located on the edge of the Mogollon highlands with easy access to higher elevation resources of the pinyon-juniper and ponderosa-pine mountain zones.

During the 1948 excavations, Bat Cave yielded a primitive, small-cob popcorn that fit expectations of what early domesticated maize in the Southwest should look like. In 1950, Dick and a research team from the University of Colorado resumed excavations. Their work was devoted to obtaining samples of wood and charcoal for radiocarbon dating. The corn itself—botanists had already agreed it was very ancient—was not dated because the process of radiocarbon dating is destructive. At that time, a relatively large sample would have been needed for dating purposes, and the corn was considered too valuable for use in comparative botanical studies to be wasted in the dating process. When the dating was finished, the results proved to be strikingly early: 6000 to 5500 B.P. (4000 to 2500 B.C.). Nowhere were the dates on maize as early as at Bat Cave, but pre-ceramic contexts for maize were also established at Swallow Cave in Chihuahua, and Cordova, Jemez, and Tularosa caves in New Mexico.

Archaeologists tried to reconstruct the manner in which corn that had been domesticated in Mexico came to the Southwest, bearing two facts in mind. First, botanical evidence pointed to corn's having been domesticated in an area of Mexico that was considerably wetter than the arid Southwest. Second, the excavated caves and rock shelters along the eastern edge of the Sierra Madre in Chihuahua and central mountains of New Mexico—and Bat Cave in particular—had produced the oldest maize known in the Southwest. The model developed suggested that maize had entered the Southwest by means of a "highland corridor" where, because of the high elevations, the climate was moist and corn could be grown without irrigation.

The very early Bat Cave dates led archaeologists to accept the idea that maize remained a small and rather unimportant addition to the food supply of southwestern societies. Groups continued to forage without building permanent houses or using pottery. Finally, since the dates from Bat Cave were so early, they led to the conclusion that maize was not grown outside the highland area for centuries, perhaps not until more drought-resistant varieties had been developed. Some archaeologists suggested that maize could not have spread beyond the Mogollon highlands until climate conditions became suitable, presumably after the end of the warm, dry Altithermal originally postulated by Ernst Antevs.

Most archaeologists accepted this basic reasoning despite a growing uneasiness about the Bat Cave radiocarbon dates for maize. Some proposed other ideas, deploying a variety of imaginative intellectual contortions to account for the acceptance of maize as essentially a "nonevent," or at the very least one that had little or no impact on people living in the Mogollon highlands or elsewhere for two to three thousand years.

In 1981 and 1983, Wirt H. Wills, then a doctoral student at the University of Michigan and now a professor at the University of New Mexico, carried out additional excavations at Bat Cave. His work has greatly changed our understanding of Bat Cave and, consequently, many of our interpretations of corn's appearance in the Southwest. Wills obtained a series of dates on the corn itself, in addition to dates on squash, beans, and charcoal. By the 1980s radiocarbon techniques produced results that were far more precise and accurate than those of the 1950s, and they required smaller samples. By the 1980s, enough southwestern maize samples had accumulated so that portions of some could be sacrificed to the dating process without jeopardizing ongoing botanical studies. The newly obtained dates cluster very tightly at 1450 B.C. (the spread is between 1491 and 970). A single date on squash of 1410 suggests that this crop was accepted at the same time as corn, a fact that has long been known. Beans date later, to about 400 B.C., also in accord with previous understanding.

The re-excavations at Bat Cave also demonstrated why the older dates were so far off the mark. Recall that these dates were not on the corn itself, but rather on associated charcoal. Wills's excavations revealed very complex cave stratigraphy in which the mixing of deposits by pack rats and mice, some very complicated geologic processes, and additional disturbance created by the construction of hearths and storage pits by Archaic foragers produced a situation in which it was extremely difficult to establish physical associations among objects. The dated charcoal showed that the cave had been used at an early period, but it did not substantiate the applicability of those dates to the corn.

In the years since Herbert Dick's first excavation at Bat Cave, many other southwestern sites containing evidence for the early cultivation of corn have been excavated and studied. These sites yield quite consistent dates that range from about 1500 B.C. to 500 B.C. Most of the dates, in fact, are between 1500 and 900. Not only are the dates in agreement, lending some credence to their accuracy, but they are gathered from maize found at sites throughout the Southwest, rather than being limited to the Mogollon and Chihuahua mountain corridor. The dates are reported on corn found in rock shelters and open sites on northern Black Mesa, Arizona, on kernels from White Dog Cave, and from two rock shelters in the San Juan Basin of New Mexico. These dates from the Colorado Plateau are particularly important, because they demonstrate that there was no lag between the acceptance of maize in the Mogollon highlands and its acceptance on the Plateau. A rock shelter in the Organ Mountains east of Las Cruces, New Mexico, is also significant because the Organ Mountains are a rugged, narrow range in the basin and range-desert grassland country, much lower in elevation than sites in the Mogollon Mountains. Just as meaningful are dates from three sites in southern Arizona. The Arizona sites, in the Tucson Basin, are also in desert grasslands at low elevations, an area that was thought to be too warm and dry for the early maize.

The new data demonstrate that maize appeared in many locations in the Southwest at about the same time, and that the cultural contexts into which maize was adopted were diverse. Excavations by Bruce Huckell, then of the University of Arizona and the Arizona State Museum, have shown that in the low desert grasslands of the Tucson Basin, Late Archaic foragers were not as mobile, at least during certain times of the year, as previously thought. They went to the trouble of building houses and storage pits that, although neither large nor durable, imply a commitment to location that was not characteristic of the earlier, more mobile foragers. Late Archaic houses also have been excavated on the Colorado Plateau. In both locales, the houses are shallow pit structures, generally more or less circular, with slightly sunken clay-lined floors and associated storage pits and caches. Excavations in cave and rock-shelter locations on Black Mesa also corroborate some earlier work in demonstrating that in Basketmaker II times, caves were used for habitation in addition to serving as a burial place. The cave sites generally have outdoor work areas, hearths, and sleeping areas in addition to storage pits or cists. As yet, there are no excavated Late Archaic houses for the central mountain regions. Instead, excavated cave sites in these central mountain regions reveal a greater intensity of occupation in the Late Archaic. Processing of plant food and storage were the most important uses of the caves at this time. Storage of corn and squash would have given Late Archaic people a backup resource, allowing them to spend more time in places where wild food sources, such as nuts and grass seed, occur. Archaeologists argue that adopting limited agriculture allowed these people to be more efficient foragers. In terms of purpose, the adoption of agriculture would be the equivalent of changing in order to remain the same.

Maize is not native to the Southwest. It was domesticated in Mexico from its wild ancestor, *teosinte*, that still grows in parts of Mexico, Guatemala, and Honduras. Maize and teosinte are very closely related genetically, are completely interfertile, and cross spontaneously in areas where they grow close to each other. Of all the world's grains, maize is the most fully domesticated in that it has most completely lost its ability to disperse seed and reproduce without human intervention. The evolution of maize and the societies that domesticated and developed it truly are intertwined.

Corn seems to have spread slowly north from Mexico, though new dates on maize from Mexico—if they can be verified—would considerably narrow the lag time between domestication of corn and its spread to the Southwest and elsewhere. At any rate, once it reached the Southwest, it dispersed rapidly throughout the region. The route over which corn was planted farther and farther north is still a matter of debate. We do know that corn was selected and modified so that a plant that had originated in the somewhat moister tropics of Mesoamerica could withstand the dry climate and short growing seasons of the Pueblo homeland. If corn had not been so fully domesticated already, the genetic changes it must have undergone would have taken many thousands of years to develop. With humans selecting certain characteristics, probably quite unconsciously, change was far more rapid.

The grain that eventually became Pueblo corn might have been planted by foraging groups who lived increasingly farther north of the tropics, where corn was first domesticated. Those plants that matured early might be harvested, with some being saved and used for seed corn in future plantings. Foragers do not spend much time in one area, so that the slower-maturing plants would be left for birds, insects, and small animals, but not replanting. By such means, corn may have diversified as it spread throughout the Americas. For example, the yellow flint corn of the Caribbean thrives at sea level, whereas Puno maize is cultivated successfully near Lake Titicaca, in the Andes, at an elevation of 12,000 feet (3800 meters) above sea level. The Chococeno maize of Colombia grows in wet, coastal areas, while varieties of Hopi corn are planted in sand dunes. The versatility of maize is reflected by the fact that today there are some 300 varieties grown worldwide.

The earliest corn varieties grown in the Southwest were small-cob popcorns of a type called Chapalote, which is still grown in parts of northern Mexico. Sometime before 500 B.C., this corn crossed, probably naturally, with teosinte to produce a hybrid. Within a few centuries, this hybrid interbred with a new introduction from Mexico—an eight-row flour corn called Harinoso de Ocho or Maiz de Ocho. From this pool of diverse corn types—present in the Southwest by 300 B.C.—all future varieties found in the region developed.

Because the genetically variable teosinte-crossed corn was amenable to human manipulation and selection, its productivity and reliability as a crop could be substantially enhanced. Human selection could also have facilitated the successful growth of different varieties of corn in many settings, including those in the low, arid, southwestern desert grasslands.

Along with maize, Pueblo ancestors planted squash, also of Mesoamerican origin. Radiocarbon dates from the Southwest indicate that squash probably was introduced at about the same time as corn. Although squash does not provide the same high nutritional value as corn, the flesh is edible when ripe, and also can be dried and stored. Squash seeds are edible and nutritious, and the rind is useful as a container and can be shaped into a variety of small tools.

The third staple of ancient American agriculture is the common bean, varieties of which we recognize as pinto, red navy, and kidney. Beans appear somewhat later in the archaeological record of the Southwest. They are present by 500 to 300 B.C. Beans are an excellent source of protein. In addition, they contain a high level of lysine, an amino acid that facilitates digestion of the protein available in corn. As legumes, beans assist in returning nitrogen to the soil so that when planted in the same fields with corn and squash, soil depletion of that key plant nutrient is ameliorated. The remarkable complementary nature of corn, beans, and squash—that Native American triumvirate—is frequently noted by botanists and nutritionists. Likely as not, the peoples who first planted these crops knew nothing about their properties. Still, the knowledge ancient Native Americans had, and their descendants still possess, of seed selection—of when, how, where, and how much to plant, and of how to store and prepare the crops for food—is in itself extraordinary.

Corn is so essential to the Pueblo way of life that it also figures prominently in ritual, ceremony, and prayer. Corn pollen is offered in prayer for fertility and is ritually fed to fetishes and other sacred paraphernalia. Cornmeal is also part of many ritual offerings, as are ears of corn. The Pueblos plant many different varieties of corn, most classified by color. At Hopi, for example, there are at least 24 varieties planted, although most of the fields are devoted to blue corn and white corn. As mentioned before, the cardinal directions are associated with colors. When, for ceremonial purposes, directions are marked on altars, ears of corn of the appropriate colors may be set out. On ceremonial occasions ears of corn are presented as gifts. A 16th-century Spanish prelate wrote about the Pueblos, "Here corn is God!" While the observation was not precisely true, it is undeniable that corn and religion are intertwined. For the Pueblos, as for other Native Americans, corn is not merely the product of human labor. It is a gift from God, a miracle for which thanks is always given.

The earliest corn grown in the Southwest was a type called Chapalote—a small-cob popcorn with 12 or 14 rows of small kernels. Sometime before 500 B.C. this corn was crossed with teosinte, a wild grass, to produce a hybrid. The teosinte shown below dates from 5000 B.C. The hybrid Balsas Teosinte, from Mexico, was the genetic forerunner of modern corn. Because the genetically variable corn could be selected and manipulated, varieties were developed by Pueblo farmers to suit many different climates and settings. Yellow flint corn, for instance, thrives at sea level, while some other varieties grow best at high elevations.

Yellow flint corn

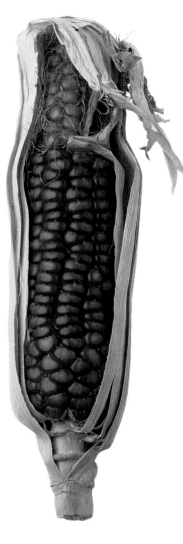

Teosinte   **Balsas Teosinte**   **Chapalote**

Corn, as a tropical grass, grows near the limits of its tolerances in the Southwest. The factors critical for its growth are the amount of water the plant receives, the length of the growing season, soil conditions (including nutrients), and safety from pests, crop diseases, and the strong winds of the spring growing season. Of these, the amount and timing of moisture during key portions of the growing season are the most critical. In the Southwest, corn has been grown successfully for millennia despite the characteristic aridity, the short growing seasons, and the unpredictable timing and amount of the rainfall. Ritual, ceremony, and prayer are therefore appropriate for those acts of God and nature over which man has no control. A great deal of Pueblo ceremony is concerned with assuring rain and the fertility of crops. In the Zuni cosmology, for example, corn is given to humans only after they have learned the ritual needed to encourage the appropriate kinds of rain—male (hard downpours) and female (gentle rain)—needed for agriculture to prosper.

Whenever human knowledge and decisions can influence the success of farming, they are used. The Pueblos have a great store of traditional technological information at their command. For example, when they select locations for planting, farmers observe key species of natural vegetation as clues to soil moisture content and fertility. They may taste the soil to see that it is not too salty. Corn is traditionally planted in low earth hills, each containing several plants, and the hills placed a few yards apart. In the Southwest, where strong spring winds are characteristic, planting in hills allows the outer plants to protect the inner ones from wind damage. The distance between hills also helps prevent pests or disease from ruining an entire field and the spatial separation of hills reduces the competition between plants for moisture. When the crop has been harvested, stalks may be left in the ground. The following year, hills are made in between those of the previous season. This kind of alternation serves as a way of fallowing that prevents soil depletion.

The cultural values and attitudes Pueblo people express are an essential part of their strategy for agricultural success. Modern varieties of hybrid corn are selected to perform under the average, rather uniform, conditions one might find in an Iowa cornfield, for example. In the Pueblo world, however, where the amount of rainfall varies dramatically, there is no advantage in adapting to a mean. Rather, selection must maintain diversity. Ethnobotanist Gary Nabhan queried an elderly Hopi woman about how seed corn was selected, wondering if seeds were saved from plants that matured earliest, or from cobs that had the truest color, or kernels that were the most uniform. The woman listened to his questions and responded, "It is not a good habit to be too picky.... We have been given this corn, small seeds, fat seeds, misshapen seeds, all of them. It would show that we are not thankful for what we have received if we plant certain of our seeds and not others."

It is difficult, if not impossible, to know the agricultural practices used prehistorically in the Southwest, but some of the techniques documented among contemporary southwestern peoples certainly reach back into ancient times. We do not now understand the process that must have taken place to produce the Hopi dune-adapted corn. This corn is distinct in that the *mescotyl*, or shoot, that develops from the root to the first foliage leaf, can reach a length of 10 to 12 inches (25 to 30 centimeters) compared to only 1.5 to 6 inches (4 to 15 centimeters) in other corn. The seed can be planted as deep as 10 inches (25 centimeters) or more within a sand dune, and the plant will still grow to the surface. Sand is a natural mulch, so that by planting in dunes, Hopi farmers allow the seed to germinate in a relatively moisture-rich environment, while the genetic composition of the plant produces a specialized form and shape that allows it to develop and grow.

Squash and beans were the other staple crops of ancient Pueblo agriculture. Squash was originally imported from Mesoamerica. Although not as nutritionally valuable as corn, squash had the same advantages: it was edible when ripe and could be dried and stored. Squash can also be used as a container. Radiocarbon testing shows that squash came into the area at about the same time as corn. Beans made their appearance later, at about 500 to 300 B.C. Beans, squash, and corn are complementary, and together form a nutritious diet. When planted in the same fields, they minimize the depletion of soil nutrients.

As Gary Nabhan has observed, we do not know how many genes differentiate the Hopi dune-adapted corn from visually similar seeds that have come from elsewhere. When Hopi blue-flour corn and visually similar, closely related Tarahumara blue-flint corn were planted experimentally in the same field, plant form, placement of cobs on the stalk, days to maturity, ear weight, and yield all turned out to be considerably different! Unlike a general tolerance for short growing seasons, these differences reflect highly specific adaptations to local conditions. It is not likely that they came about by casual selection.

Careful selection of field locations also helps ensure sufficient water for corn. Fields may be placed in areas of deep soils with good moisture-retaining properties; on slopes exposed to the north or east, which receive less direct solar radiation and therefore hold moisture; within stream flood plains or the mouths of arroyos (ephemeral streams), which are naturally irrigated; or in sand dunes that act as a mulch. When corn is planted in locations without subsurface moisture, water from rainfall runoff or from streams or springs may be diverted at critical points in the growing season.

Modern hybrid corn requires a growing season of about 120 days, a condition that is available throughout most of the Southwest. When corn is grown under dry conditions, however, it matures slowly and may need a growing season of 130 to 140 days. If more moisture can be made available to the crop, then the length of the growing season is much less critical. Some of the planting strategies that help to increase the amount of water available to corn are not appropriate to ensure an adequately long growing season. For example, the growing season on north- and east-facing slopes is generally considerably shorter than on south- and west-facing slopes. The dual problems of inadequate moisture and short growing seasons may be compensated for by

Corn was so important to Pueblo life that it became part of ritual, ceremony, and prayers. Many varieties, most distinguished by color, have been selected and developed. Two dozen are planted at Hopi, with white and blue dominating. During ceremonies, ears of corn of the appropriate color are placed on altars to mark the cardinal directions (red for south and southeast; blue for west and southwest; white for east and northeast; yellow for north and northwest; and black for above). At other Pueblos, the colors denote different directions.

Hopi red corn   Hopi blue corn   Hopi white corn

planting fields in a variety of topographic settings, as the Hopi do today. Hopi fields are planted at different elevations, at various locations along arroyos, across arroyos, and in arroyo terraces. Additionally, crops may be planted at different times in the season so that some harvest will be obtained even if there is a late spring or early autumn frost. Finally, different varieties of corn are grown; some are adapted to drought conditions, some to short growing seasons, and some to strong winds. Maintaining these varieties is usually accomplished by wide spatial separation of fields. Dispersing fields also decreases the chance of complete crop failure. Even if some fields are ruined by too much or too little rainfall, for instance, other fields may not be affected as much.

The kinds of agricultural practices and strategies that will ensure productive growth of corn in the Southwest—planting in different locations, multiple plantings during the growing season, careful selection of seed corn, maintaining the separation of different varieties of corn, and the diversion of water to crops when necessary during critical periods of the growing season—all require a substantial investment in time and energy. A truism of farming in the Southwest is that, given enough energy, care, and effort, corn can be grown nearly everywhere. But in order for the necessary care to be given people must remain in the vicinity of their crops, at least during the growing season.

The restriction on mobility leads us to appreciate patterns noted in the archaeological record. Recent archaeological work has revealed evidence of houses and storage facilities in association with the earliest radiocarbon dates on corn. This suggests that the Late Archaic peoples who accepted agriculture were not quite the widely ranging mobile foragers of earlier periods. Possibly because regional populations had reached critical levels for the continued support of highly mobile groups or because climatic changes had decreased the regional productivity of large zones within the Southwest (as would have occurred with a dry and widespread Altithermal), the groups that became agricultural may have begun to store foods to tide them over times when they no longer had access to abundant wild food sources.

When crops are grown successfully, stores can be maintained and used when necessary, perhaps throughout the winter, but particularly in late winter and early spring, when the availability of wild foods is at its lowest. A supply of seed corn adequate for the next planting must be stored as well. Corn is quite easily stored without much preparation. Ease of storing and caching is not an advantage for highly mobile groups, but it is of critical importance when people stay in the same place for any length of time. As agriculture became increasingly important, an even greater investment of time and energy devoted to storage facilities and more substantial residences would be certain to pay off. In the Southwest, pottery containers and domestic architecture that incorporated space for storage became regional hallmarks and the criteria by which archaeologists recognize the origins and development of regional traditions.

The Hopi plant their corn at different elevations and locations and at different times, ensuring that some plants will survive the variable and often difficult growing conditions of the Southwest. The Hopi also maintain many varieties of corn, each tolerant of slightly different climatic and soil conditions. These measures cut down the odds of a total crop loss should there be too much or too little rainfall or an early or late frost.

Although we cannot be certain of prehistoric agricultural practices, we can learn much from the modern Pueblos. The Hopi plant a dune-adapted corn plant that produces a shoot almost three times as long as in other varieties. The seed can be planted deep within the dune, yet still reach the surface. When dunes form over relatively impervious subsoil or rock—as they do at Hopi—the sand acts as a mulch, retaining moisture and allowing the seed to germinate. The length of the shoot allows the plant to reach sunlight.

Had the Southwest not been an area in which pottery was used, its prehistory as described by archaeologists would have been vastly different. Archaeologists have named more than 600 pottery types. They use these types as indicators of cultural affiliation and, having ordered changes in pottery types over time, as temporal markers as well. Essentially though, pottery is made to be useful, as containers for cooking, storing, and serving foods and liquids. Pottery appeared in the Southwest when the lifestyle of the people became somewhat sedentary. Ceramic containers, because they are both heavy and fragile, are not useful items for highly mobile groups, especially those without pack animals.

Ceramic vessels are, however, advantageous for storing either liquids or dry foods, and because they may be sealed easily with stone or clay covers, their contents can be kept safe from the depredations of insects and rodents. Sealed pots also protect dry food from water. Pottery vessels may be made more

The varieties of corn and the technology for growing them under difficult conditions may be the most enduring legacy the Pueblo peoples have given the world. Maize has gone from being a staple crop of Native Americans to one of the four principal food plants on the planet.

quickly than baskets, and unlike baskets they will not become fragile with age. Although baskets can be woven very tightly and then coated with pitch or other substances to make them watertight, pottery is still more versatile for cooking. Pottery vessels may be left untended for long periods over a low fire or a bed of coals while the contents simmer or are reheated. This can be a great advantage when other tasks compete for time with cooking and preparing meals. On a worldwide basis, pottery is most often associated with peoples who are more, rather than less, sedentary and who live in regions where there are long stretches of sunny days that allow clay vessels to cure and dry before they are fired. The Southwest became an ideal region for pottery production and use, once stored food—which included corn—precluded a way of life based on foraging and high mobility.

The earliest settlements in the Pueblo homeland were very small hamlets rather than villages. Settlements may consist of a score or so houses, but it is likely that not all were occupied at the same time. Rather, settlement locations were used over and over again, probably by the same groups of people. Some communities were occupied seasonally. At Black Mesa, for example, winter habitation sites in upland areas were fairly substantial. Smaller settlements, probably little more than camping places, were used in summer. The reoccupation of settlement locations, the use of storage facilities, burial caves, and houses all suggest considerable changes in organization and social life from the kinds of patterns one would expect with the highly mobile foraging populations of the Early and Middle Archaic. Yet full Pueblo village life did not occur simultaneously with the appearance of agriculture.

When the first Spaniards ventured north into the Southwest, they were greatly impressed with Pueblo agriculture and foods. Pedro de Castañeda, a chronicler of the Coronado expeditions in 1540, wrote of Zuni, "The Indians plant in holes, and the corn does not grow tall, but each stalk bears three or four ears with 800 grains each ..." In the 1580 accounts of the Hopi, the Spaniards noted the people could plant in sandy places because the moisture from snow was carefully guarded.

The first Spaniards to see the Pueblos along the Rio Grande wrote that the river "... flows through a broad valley planted with fields of maize.... There are twelve pueblos. The houses are of mud, two stories high. The people seem good, more given to farming than to war. They have provisions of maize, beans, melons." Castañeda writes of the Pueblos of the Rio Grande:

> The men spin and weave; the women take care of the children and prepare the food. The land is so fertile that they need to cultivate only once a year, just for planting, for the snow falls and covers the fields, and the maize grows under the snow. In one year they harvest enough for seven years.

Farther to the east, Pecos Pueblo, on the boundary between the Pueblo world and the Great Plains, was described by a Spanish chronicler of the 16th century:

> This pueblo had five plazas. It was also provided with such an abundant supply of corn that everyone marveled. There were those who maintained that the total must amount to more than thirty thousand *fanegas* [a dry volume measure equal to about 16 gallons, or 50 liters] since each house had two or three rooms full of it, all of excellent quality. Moreover, there was a good supply of beans. Both corn and beans were of many colors; it seemed that some of the corn was two or three years old.

The downside of the Spanish conquerors' evident admiration for this agricultural abundance is that they—particularly the soldiers—took whatever they wanted from the pueblos, even if it harmed the Indians. Yet the varieties of Pueblo maize, and the Pueblo technology for growing corn and other crops, may be the most important gifts they have to give to humankind. From being the staple grain crop of the Americas, maize has joined wheat, rice, and potatoes as one of the four principal food plants worldwide. In the over-populated 20th-century world, where drought produces suffering and starvation for millions of people who cannot afford high-technology agriculture and for whom mono-cropping agribusiness would be a disastrous failure, Pueblo maize, Pueblo knowledge of cultivation, and Pueblo ability to maintain the genetic diversity of crops may substantially change the odds in favor of human survival.

For most of their history, the Mogollon lived in small settlements of semisubterranean pithouses. After about A.D. 550 they moved their settlements
cent to streams and rivers where the land was arable. As this reconstruction shows, the houses of this period were rectangular and were built in

4

THE EMERGENCE OF THE MOGOLLON

Don Juan Ignacio Flores Mogollón, governor of the Province of New Mexico from 1712 to 1715, is credited with having discovered the rich mineral deposits—principally copper and silver—that are scattered throughout the vast region of rugged mountains in southwestern New Mexico that bear his name. The governor's name has also been given to the ancient Native American inhabitants of the area, none of whom ever used the metals at their disposal. Prehistoric Mogollon culture was discovered and

from ridges and high bluffs to lower ground adjacent groups without any apparent settlement plan.

The Mogollon inhabited a vast tract of largely mountainous territory in what is now New Mexico, Arizona, and the Mexican states of Chihuahua and Sonora. Mogollon tradition has been defined on the basis of dark red and brown pottery and the construction of pithouse dwellings. Some of the most important discoveries of both pottery and pithouses have been made in the Mimbres Valley area of southwest New Mexico.

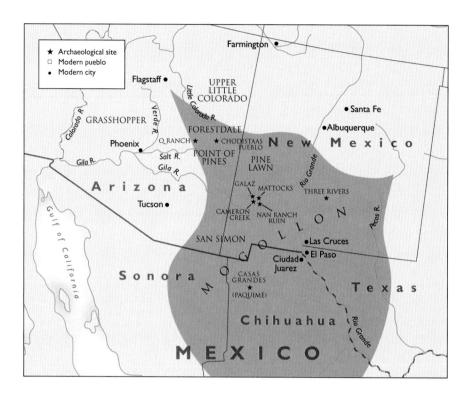

named by archaeologist Emil Haury, who conducted the first excavations of Mogollon settlements between 1931 and 1936.

The people who left behind the relics that archaeologists term Mogollon did not use writing, so the name they called themselves, whether or not they spoke a single language or believed that they were all one people, must forever be unknown. The Mogollon tradition is recognized on the basis of two of the most durable classes of archaeological material: pottery and architecture. Once the Late Archaic peoples of the Mogollon Mountains began to depend on corn, they spent weeks near their fields each year. Pottery vessels, even though heavy and breakable, thus became very useful as containers for cooking and for storing water and grain. Unpainted pottery normally was brown in color, but the distinguishing Mogollon ceramics are dark red and brown wares. The need to stay in one place for prolonged periods of the year naturally encouraged the construction of shelters; in the case of the Mogollon, the pithouse was the standard dwelling form. Some other cultural practices were also relatively constant among the Mogollon. For example, although corn agriculture was present from the Late Archaic, hunting continued to be a major economic activity, with gathering persisting, but of decidedly less importance.

The first pottery and pithouses of the Mogollon region date to about A.D. 200. The period from A.D. 200 to about 550 is referred to as the Early Pithouse period. A Late Pithouse period lasted from 550 to about 1000, when there was a change from pithouses to above-ground pueblo dwellings. In some locations, the Mogollon tradition lasted in a coherent form until about 1450. In other parts of the Mogollon region, there occurred a major change at about A.D. 1130. Today, the biological descendants of the Mogollon are very likely living among the modern residents of the Pueblo of Zuni and the several Hopi villages.

Mogollon country, where brown ware pottery and pithouses occur together, extends from an eastern border near the Guadalupe Mountains, between Carlsbad and Las Cruces, New Mexico, west to the Verde River of central Arizona and from the Little Colorado River on the north to central Chihuahua and Sonora, Mexico, on the south. This is an enormous territory—more than twice the size of even the most generous estimates of the Colorado Plateau country occupied by the Anasazi, the northern and more widely known neighbors of the Mogollon.

Much of Mogollon country is mountainous. The volcanic Mogollon Mountains rise to an elevation of 10,770 feet (3300 meters). Intermontaine basins drop well below 3000 feet (900 meters). Patches of alpine meadow are found at the highest elevations, while cactus, sparse desert grasses and shrubs dominate the lowest basins. At the elevations in between, ponderosa pine forest occurs above 6000 feet (1800 meters), and mixed pinyon-juniper woodland and oak chaparral below. Even today, the extremely rugged terrain makes east to west travel difficult.

Given the immense size of the area, its diverse and rugged landscapes, the difficulty of transport and consequent isolation of the intermontaine basins and valleys, it is no surprise that different cultural subtraditions developed at their own pace within the region. Archaeologists recognize these by giving separate subregions of the Mogollon their own names: Chihuahua, Forestdale, Grasshopper, Jornada, Mimbres, Pine Lawn, Point of Pines, Q Ranch, San Simon, and Upper Little Colorado.

The kinds of changes archaeologists recognize as evidence of different stages in Mogollon cultural development are rather subtle. For example, in the Early Pithouse period, settlements are often located on ridges or mesa tops, and the pithouses are circular. During the same period, Mogollon pottery took the form of plain, unpainted brown ware. During the Late Pithouse period, from about A.D. 600 to 900, both valley floors and higher landforms were used and the pithouses were rectangular. Storage and serving vessels were made from red-slipped pottery (slip is a pure clay that provides a smooth surface and color) and pottery that was decorated with red paint on a brownish background. Cooking pots, of course, continued to be unpainted. The dead were buried in simple pits dug in the ground outside of dwellings, inside abandoned rooms, and under the floors of occupied rooms. Somewhat later and at different times throughout the Mogollon region, though generally about A.D. 1000, people began to live above ground in houses arranged in pueblos with contiguous rooms and plazas. In some areas black-on-white pottery was produced. Also in some locations, burials beneath the floors of occupied rooms became the consistent pattern. These changes did not occur at a uniform rate throughout

Mogollon territory, but within the smaller subregions the timing of change was more homogeneous.

Here we will concentrate on specific sites and locales in order to examine the major features of the Mogollon region more closely and to highlight, as much as is possible, the organization of Mogollon society. The bulk of archaeological surveys and excavations have been focused on the Mimbres, Reserve, and Pine Lawn areas of New Mexico and the Grasshopper and Q Ranch subregions of Arizona. The Mogollon region is so vast—and much of it is so rugged—that, as incredible as it may seem in the last decade of the 20th century, major portions of the region are as yet poorly known in archaeological terms.

Late Archaic sites have yielded maize, evidence of dwellings, and burials that indicate the beginnings of an agricultural economy and a more sedentary way of life. The Mogollon tradition begins with the addition of pottery to this base. The earliest Mogollon pottery, from the Pine Lawn area, is undecorated brown or red/brown ware. The clays used were generally alluvial in origin and did not require the addition of temper. Vessels were built up by coiling, then shaped and finished by scraping the coiled surfaces smooth. Sometimes, a small smooth stone was also used to further polish the vessel's exterior. The most common vessel forms are jars, necked jars, small seed jars, and bowls.

Even the earliest pottery is technically competent. There is no hint that the potters were learning as they worked, or that they were experimenting with a new medium. This is to be expected because the Late Archaic predecessors of the Mogollon had acquired considerable experience with clay used to line hearths, the floors of dwellings, and storage pits. Furthermore, any real disasters in shaping could be broken down and returned to raw clay before the vessels were fired. Even today, Pueblo potters fire their pottery in the open without a kiln, as did their Mogollon and Anasazi ancestors. It is difficult to maintain consistent temperatures with open firing, and sudden gusts of wind can mean that vessels will crack and break. It is probable that in the past, just as today, these firing accidents would not be brought home from the firing area. Early experiments with pottery are unlikely to become part of the archaeological record because archaeologists normally excavate houses and settlements where it is unusual to find either shaping mistakes or pottery broken in firing.

The earliest Mogollon settlements, also from the Pine Lawn and the Mimbres areas, date from about A.D. 200 to 550. These contained from one to as many as 80 pithouses, although it is likely that only a few of the pithouses in the larger settlements were occupied at any one time. Pithouse dwellings were sunken—some portion of their walls were also the sides of an excavated pit. The depth to which pithouse floors were excavated varies. Generally speaking, the floors extended just below the frost line, which is determined by the latitude and elevation of the site—about 18 inches (45 centimeters) in much of the Mogollon area. The sunken floor pithouse design is thermally efficient, in part because of the insulating properties of the ground.

The broken terrain around the Mogollon Rim is typical of the harsh surroundings in which the Mogollon people lived.

Pithouses required less heat in winter to keep them moderately warm than did surface structures of similar size.

Initially, pithouse communities were located on prominent ridges, high bluffs, or isolated knolls, often with rock walls across the most accessible route to the settlement. Below these hamlets, there was generally good agricultural land, often a river floodplain. Later, after about A.D. 550, pithouse settlements were moved to lower ground adjacent to streams or rivers and good arable land. The settings of early pithouse settlements may be a reflection of a need for defense.

Residents of the early pithouse communities may have had to defend their food supply from raiding parties, either from hunter-gatherers or other early farmers. The mountainous Mogollon region is favorable for hunting and it continued to be an important aspect of Mogollon subsistence throughout the prehistoric period. Early Mogollon hamlets arose in the same areas where other groups of people continued a hunting and gathering way of life, since there is no reason to suppose that everyone in the Southwest or the Mogollon region itself adopted agriculture at the same time. It is plausible, then, that small communities with enough agricultural produce to store over a season felt threatened by potential raids from neighboring hunters and gatherers. Alternatively, it has been suggested that farming in the Mogollon mountains would have been very risky because of short growing seasons and variable rainfall. Communities might wish to protect their stores from potentially aggressive agricultural neighbors whose crops had failed.

Early Mogollon houses were roundish pithouses, from 10 to 16 feet (3 to 5 meters) in diameter, excavated to depths ranging from 2 to 5 feet (0.6 to 1.5 meters). Roofs were either an umbrella type, with a central upright post serving as the main support, or they were domed with the beams supported by marginal posts. The roofs themselves were made of thick logs covered by branches and layers of mud. An entry was on one side. By about A.D. 600, the Mogollon built pithouses that were rectangular in shape with the side entryway including a ramp constructed to slope upward to the ground surface. Three or more sturdy upright posts supported the roof. The early pithouses generally have one or more large interior subfloor storage pits. In later pithouses, these are less common, possibly because pottery vessels assumed a large part of the storage function.

Not all of the early pithouses have interior hearths. Some cooking was done outdoors, but the dwellings without hearths or ash-filled warming pits may not have been occupied in the coldest part of the year. Some families may have used rock shelters during the winter months. Household equipment and furnishings from rock shelter sites include grass beds, rabbit fur or bird feather blankets, plant-fiber scouring pads, fire drills, fire tongs, metates, and manos. The presence of central fire hearths is a more consistent feature of the later pithouse period.

By modern standards, most early Mogollon settlements were tiny. Settlements with a momentary occupation of four to six dwellings would have had a population of about 30 men, women, and children—too small a number either to guarantee marriage partners or provide access to the kind of diverse resources that might have been needed to offset a poor harvest or hunting season. A larger group must have interacted on a fairly regular basis. A sense of just such a larger community can be glimpsed in the construction of special structures used by groups of people from different households. Archaeologists refer to these structures as kivas because of their special—probably ritual—functions, and by analogy to similar structures in all modern pueblos.

Among the Mogollon, three different community patterns developed. At some of the moderate- to larger-sized pithouse sites that have been excavated, one or more oversized communal kiva structures have been found. Sometimes these larger structures also have distinctive shapes and features, such as "lobes" constructed around the entryway. This arrangement of several pithouses and one community structure is apparent at the SU site near Reserve, New Mexico. SU (the name derives from a local cattle brand) contained at least 26 houses.

A second pattern is reflected in the many pithouse settlements that consist of only two or three spatially dispersed houses. Settlements of this type are common in the more mountainous central and western portions of the Mogollon region such as Forestdale and Point of Pines. In settlements of this type, all of the houses appear to have been used for normal residential functions, but there generally was a large or "great" kiva. The great kiva is physically set apart from the domestic structures, but is also approximately central to the scattered dwellings.

A third pattern is noted in the Grasshopper region and perhaps elsewhere in the northern Mogollon subregions. In this instance, small settlements are dispersed over the landscape, but the largest have a separate great kiva that may have been used by all the inhabitants of the area. The term focal community serves to indicate the social centrality of the settlements with great kivas. Typically, among Mogollon pithouse settlements of all varieties, there is no indication that houses are arranged other than in a haphazard or convenient fashion or in any particular relationship to one another. There appears to have been no settlement plan.

In general, the long period from about A.D. 550 to 950 witnessed great stability in the Mogollon area. Hunting and some gathering continued to be important even though agriculture was widely adopted. Early pithouses were large enough to shelter an extended family that may have been the unit of cooperative farming, hunting, and gathering. Many settlements seem to have consisted of only one or a very few families. Later pithouses are smaller, but each settlement has more structures, suggesting perhaps that the basic cooperating group was the nuclear family, several of which occupied the same hamlet.

Pottery that initially had been only unpainted, rough, plain ware was decorated later in the period. A highly polished red slip was used on some vessels. Others were painted with red designs on a brown background. Once settlements in defensive settings were abandoned and pithouses were built close to arable land, Mogollon culture presents an almost static picture for nearly 400 years, a period when the population grew, new communities formed, people continued to farm, gather, hunt, and engage in whatever rituals and ceremonies were needed to thank the gods for peace, food, and the health of their children.

Household articles such as the mano and metate shown here have been found both in pithouses and in the rock shelters that some families may have used during winter months. Manos and metates were used for grinding corn and indicate a growing dependence on agriculture.

Sometime between A.D. 1000 and 1150, three major changes occurred. Taken together, these are so striking that early investigators concluded that settlements built after the changes were not Mogollon at all, but a regional variant of the Anasazi. The first and most obvious change was in the nature of the dwellings built. Mogollon residences evolved from pithouses to above-ground pueblos with contiguous, rectangular rooms and open areas or plazas. Secondly, the long-established brown or red ware Mogollon pottery was replaced by clay vessels painted black on white. Thirdly, although much more difficult to reconstruct, the population increased and expanded into less productive agricultural areas.

Among the Mogollon of the Mimbres Valley of New Mexico, especially, the cobble masonry that is found in the above-ground pueblo rooms is particularly rough. Some have compared it, unkindly, to stacked ball bearings. In the 1950s and 1960s, archaeologists interpreted the Mimbres Mogollon's unrefined masonry as evidence that building in stone was a newly acquired skill. Because their Anasazi neighbors had already been building masonry pueblos for some 150 to 200 years, these archaeologists concluded that the Anasazi had introduced masonry construction to the Mogollon. The Anasazi also decorated their painted pottery with black designs on a white background, a fact that also supported the notion that the Mogollon learned to make black-on-white vessels from the Anasazi. The combined effect of the change in domestic architecture and pottery decoration led to the suggestion that the Mogollon somehow had been taken over by the Anasazi. Indeed some scholars argued that after A.D. 1000, the Mogollon had ceased to exist as a cultural entity separate from the Anasazi.

A discussion of Mogollon developments in the Grasshopper and Q Ranch regions of central Arizona provides an example of these developments in a well-studied area. North of the upper Salt River, the Grasshopper and Q Ranch areas occupy rugged adjacent high plateaus and their associated canyons. The high elevations and aridity of the regions make successful farming an uncertain proposition. Today much of the area lies within the Cibeque Apache Reservation, where the use of irrigation has made farming successful. But irrigation was not used by the prehistoric Mogollon of the same area. As occurred elsewhere, the early Mogollon settlements in these regions are located on defensible, high landforms overlooking arable lands. Based on scant occupational debris, it is considered likely that settlement was either seasonal or very short term. Later settlements are established in valley floors and closer to potential garden areas, although these too are thought to have been occupied only seasonally. Throughout the area, settlements are very small, consisting of one or a few scattered pithouses. Settlements with several dwellings may also have had an oversized great kiva. According to University of Arizona archaeologist J. Jefferson Reid, who has made an intensive study of the Grasshopper region, these were focal communities, because they probably served as centers for the highly dispersed and still considerably mobile population.

Locally made brown wares were used for cooking, but during the period between about A.D. 600 and 1150, there is an interesting patterning in non-local ceramics that suggest changing interactions with external regions over time. At the beginning of the period, both painted ware and some plain ware were imported from the Lower Sonoran Desert of Arizona where a non-Pueblo people, whom archaeologists call Hohokam, resided. By the end of the period, Hohokam ceramics of the Lower Sonoran Desert no longer occur in the area, but Anasazi trade wares are found. Investigators propose a number of interpretations to account for the presence of Hohokam pottery in the area. Some have suggested that two different ethnic groups, Hohokam and Mogollon, were coresident in the region. Others propose highly transient use of the region by peoples of different geographic origin. Finally, a third perspective is that local peoples interacted with outsiders through informal exchange networks.

The transition from pithouse to pueblo occurs in the Grasshopper and Q Ranch regions between about 1000 and 1150. Initially, small pueblos are thinly scattered on the landscape. During the 1200s, there are larger pueblos in the adjacent region of Point of Pines, but only small pueblos in the Q Ranch area. Reid suggests that most small settlements consisting of a few cobble masonry surface rooms may have been used on a seasonal basis or, if used continuously, only for a few years at a time. After 1200, the masonry was mainly composed of dressed stone similar to Anasazi building techniques. Both great kivas and smaller kivas in the same settlement suggest the continuation of a pattern of focal communities, which serve a highly dispersed population.

The ceramics associated with these sites continue to be Mogollon brown wares. Locally made red-slipped types also were used. Painted black-on-white types, however, seem exclusively to be imports, occurring in small number, from the Anasazi region just northward in the vicinity of Zuni and the Rio Puerco. These are the Cibola white wares such as Puerco, Snowflake, and Reserve Black-on-white. In contrast to the Mimbres Valley, discussed in detail below, population numbers seem to have remained small and there was no development of a local black-on-white pottery tradition.

The period between A.D. 1150 and 1350 was one of dramatic change throughout the Southwest. A brief summary of the Grasshopper region will serve as an example. Chodistaas Pueblo, an 18-room site located on a bluff, was constructed between 1263 and the 1280s. The walls of Chodistaas were made of dressed masonry, in Anasazi rather than Mogollon mode. A great variety of painted ceramic styles in black-on-white pottery are represented at Chodistaas. These probably were not manufactured locally, but Reid doubts that Chodistaas was a large enough settlement to have attracted significant trade. Rather, he suggests that the ceramic diversity reflects either movement of people to the area or, possibly, ethnic coresidence. Eventually, Chodistaas itself, and two other excavated communities of approximately the same size in the region, were burned. The final coming together of population at Grasshopper took place between 1275 and 1400 and seems to have involved a population increase deriving in large part from dislocations caused by Anasazi populations abandoning the Plateau during the Great Drought of 1277 to 1299.

In the Mimbres subregion of Mogollon territory, the dwelling form changed from pithouse to above-ground pueblos at about A.D. 1000. Slightly before this change, the Mimbres Mogollon modified the color

scheme of their pottery first to red paint on a white ground, then to black on white. Excavations of Mimbres sites have demonstrated precedents for the masonry and evidence of in-place development of the decorated pottery styles leading to the new, and now generally accepted, view that the Mimbres Mogollon developed both stone pueblo architecture and black-on-white pottery on their own or with minimal outside influence. The evidence for gradual modification and continuity has been hard to come by because the Mimbres Valley has long been a battleground between professional archaeologists and looters.

From a European-American perspective, perhaps the most striking feature of the Mimbres Classic period (A.D. 1000 to 1130) is the production of the pottery of the same name. Art historian and anthropologist J. J. Brody describes Classic Mimbres Black-on-white pottery as less than graceful either in its forms or fabrication. A frequently warped hemispherical bowl is the most common form. Slips are grayish or muddy white as often as they are pure white. The paint color can be red, red-brown, brown, or black. Fire clouds (dark smudges produced during firing when burning fuel touches the vessel) are common. Yet, the Mimbres potter used the interior surface of bowls as a canvas for wonderfully skilled and elegant paintings. As Brody writes in his book, *Mimbres Painted Pottery*:

> With limited technical means but deft skill, using only a few compositional systems and fewer elements, these artists organized and reorganized their concave picture spaces into a myriad of complex patterns. At their worst they produced moderately pleasing decorations; at their best, powerful statements of that mysterious decorative-expressive duality that we call art.

Unfortunately for our understanding of Mogollon cultural development and the ways in which Mimbres Classic bowls were produced and used in day-to-day life, the ancient art form has attained a commercial value that jeopardizes any information about the people who made it. By the 1960s, Mimbres Classic pottery was fetching substantial sums of money on the international art market.

Most of the known painted bowls were recovered from grave sites. The Mimbres Mogollon typically inverted a bowl over the head of the deceased. The usual burial pattern during the Mimbres Classic was to place the corpse under the floor of an occupied room. In order to reach the valuable bowls, modern commercial looters used heavy equipment to dig through houses to gain access to the subfloor burials. In doing so, of course, they obliterated archaeological sites in a matter of hours. We do not know how many Classic Mimbres bowls were made. Knowledgeable sources estimate that there may be as many as 10,000 in public and private collections around the world. This astounding figure is testimony to the devastation of archaeological sites in the Mimbres Valley of New Mexico and to the destruction of vital information these sites might have provided about the daily lives of the Mimbres people.

Although the loss is irreparable, an innovative strategy to deal with the problem has been developed by archaeologist Steven LeBlanc, and has yielded some positive results. In 1974, LeBlanc founded a private and non-profit organization called the Mimbres Archaeological Center that salvaged information about Mimbres sites and established a photographic archive of known collections of Mimbres pottery. The center conducted important work at places such as the Galaz Site, the Mattocks Site, Cameron Creek Ruin, and others that had been excavated early on by amateurs and/or devastated by looters. The center also helped to focus public attention on the problem of looting, which was essential to New Mexico's passage of legislation that prohibited the willful destruction of sites on private as well as state lands. The Mimbres Archaeological Center eventually ceased its activities, but its example became the impetus for the founding of the Archaeological Conservancy. Modeled after the Nature Conservancy, the Archaeological Conservancy raises funds to acquire threatened archaeological sites; these are then deeded to those agencies that manage and protect invaluable cultural resources.

Information gleaned from the sites studied by the Mimbres Center provides partial answers to our questions about the transition of the Mogollon from pithouse to above-ground dwellers. Archaeologist Patricia Gilman noted that continuity between the pithouse and pueblo dwellers is reflected in the archaeology. Site location is an important component of that connection. Virtually all Classic Mimbres pueblos have earlier pithouse components underneath them.

Gilman also compared Mimbres pithouse architecture with a sample of house forms from around the world. She argued that together with population growth and increasing dependence on agriculture, a variety of factors would encourage a shift from pithouse architecture to above-ground pueblos. One such factor is that as more time went into the preparation of food, there arose a greater need for special, rather than shared, cooking space. Another factor was the need to store grain in increasingly large spaces that were secure, dry, and relatively insect free.

Gilman's study did not address the change from red-on-brown to black-on-white pottery. Yet here, too, there is continuity. Technologically, Mimbres Classic pottery is not a gray paste ware like that produced by the Anasazi. Rather, it is a brown ware like earlier Mogollon pottery. Only the slip is white or more often grayish or brownish. During the Late Pithouse period, before A.D. 1000, a similar pottery type was made, but it was decorated with red paint on a white slip. Slightly later, also before A.D. 1000, pithouse dwellers were producing a black-on-white ware that was technologically identical to Mimbres Classic but differed from it in decorative style. The technology and stylistic changes that occurred in the manufacture of Late Pithouse ceramics are clear evidence of an in-place development of Classic Mimbres pottery, rather than the result of changes imposed by the Anasazi.

A gradual transition from Mimbres pithouse to surface architecture has been noted at many sites but carefully studied at very few. Archaeologist Harry Shafer clearly describes this change from excavations at the NAN Ranch Ruin, a Mimbres site in southwestern New Mexico that he and his students from Texas A & M University have been studying since 1978. The NAN Ranch Ruin is exceptional among Mimbres sites in having well-preserved surface architecture. This advantage has enabled more detailed reconstruction of building sequences and events than has been possible at other Mimbres sites. Shafer describes four stages in the transition from pithouse to above-ground pueblo architecture that occurred between A.D. 925 and 1070.

In the first stage at NAN, and other Mimbres Valley sites, late pithouses are rectangular with ramp entryways. Circular clay-lined hearths with deflector stones are located between the center of the room and the ramp. Toward the end of the Late Pithouse period, Modified pithouses were built with walls lined with river cobbles. A cobble-and-adobe wall was built across the ramp entryway, closing it off, and at the same time, a hatch entry was opened in the roof. A rectangular shape was used for hearths and these were completely or partially framed by stone slabs.

Slightly later, rooms with sunken floors were constructed. The dead were now consistently buried in a flexed position in pits under the sunken floor but well away from the central activity areas of the hatchway and the rectangular hearth. Finally, all of these aspects of room configuration and building materials were retained in the surface pueblo rooms. In fact, sometimes sunken floor rooms were retained as part of the surface pueblo.

Unlike the pithouses before them, surface rooms serve a variety of functions. Living rooms have a central, rectangular, slab-lined hearth, air vents, well-prepared floors, and several roof support posts. Smaller rooms, lacking hearths and other features, are thought to have been used as storerooms.

At the NAN Ranch Ruin, archaeologists were able to determine the sequence in which rooms were built by using the uniquely well-preserved architectural stratigraphy and tree-ring, radiocarbon, archaeomagnetic and obsidian hydration dates. The archaeologists defined households as those rooms that were built during the same construction episode and joined by interior doorways. Doorways were not always present between all rooms that were constructed at the same time, and none of the doorways led to outside space. Entry to each household was by means of a hatchway in the roof. The typical household clusters at NAN Ranch Ruin consist of one large living room and most often one, but occasionally two, connecting storage rooms.

The arrangement of community space in the surface pueblos suggests continuity with the Late Pithouse villages. The settlement contains clusters of contiguous rooms, open courtyard and plaza areas, but in no particular arrangement. Placement of room blocks is haphazard. Ceremonial or communal architecture does not reflect change in community organization. Great kivas were used during the beginning of the period, but apparently were abandoned before the end. There is evidence that some small rooms were used for ritual activities. Some of these were semisubterranean and equipped with air shafts to the surface. This form of room resembles the kivas of the Anasazi area. Other particularly large surface rooms may also have been centers of ceremonial activity. Both Shafer and LeBlanc note that courtyard space may have been used for some ceremonial aspects considered appropriate for all community members to witness, as is the case in the modern Pueblo villages.

Shafer agrees with Gilman that many of the changes involved in the transition from pithouse to pueblo are explicable in technological, functional, and economic terms. Differentiation of space into rooms for storage and rooms for general living, for example, can be attributed to an increased dependence on agriculture. But Shafer also suggests that some of the specific features of the change in the Mimbres area may be related to symbolism and ideological considerations. He notes that in folk culture around the world, house form can incorporate symbols important to a people's world view. Some of the ideological factors, in turn, can be linked to characteristics of the designs on Classic Mimbres pottery.

Specifically, Shafer suggests that the Mimbres people shared a belief system that included a multilayered universe, the emergence of humans from an underworld, and aspects of ancestor worship. The architectural reflection of the multilayered universe is found in the ceiling hatchway and the placement of the dead under room floors. Passage up a ladder and through the hatchway then reenacts and symbolically represents the emergence from an underworld. Interment of the dead with a pot, perforated by a small hole, inverted over the individual's head may then symbolize a path for the individual's spirit to pass from the netherworld into the upper world as a Mimbres ancestor. Shafer notes that the Mimbres Classic style that occurs with these burials has a bordering or framing line as a consistent feature and agrees with interpretations that view the framing lines as symbolic representations of the division between worlds in the multilayered universe.

Other attributes of Mimbres painted pottery can only be guessed at. In his study, Brody found that geometric designs occur on bowls and other forms, such as jars and ladles; about half the known Mimbres painted bowls carry geometric paintings. Representational paintings occur only on bowls. On more than half of these, there is only a single figure, which may be animal, human, or a mythic being combining attributes of both. Some bowls have two, or far more rarely, three or more painted figures. On only about 15 percent of known bowls with representational paintings are the paintings narrative. In the narrative scenes, figures have some relationship to events, to narrative content, to each other, and to an imaginary environment.

Birds figure prominently on Mimbres painted pottery, as they do on later Pueblo ceramics. While simple interpretations of the images on the bowls below, such as turkeys feeding on a centipede or a man trapping birds in a garden, may be apparent to us, the references may in fact be very different. One archaeologist suggests that the man and birds may be a reference to a widespread myth involving a hero who saves the stars by trapping the crows that were eating them.

In an early style of Mimbres painted pottery called **Boldface Black-on-white** *(left)*, single-animal figures and complex, bold, symmetrical, and geometrical designs are the most characteristic features. Mimbres pottery has most often been found with burials, typically with a hole punched in the center, as on the serving vessels shown below. In excavations of Mimbres graves, archaeologists have recovered the missing center pieces, indicating that hole-punching was part of a grave-side ritual. The paired insects and deer with fish below their hooves may be allegorical figures of a now forgotten traditional history.

The vessels shown here were found at Casa Malapais, a 14th-century Mogollon village near Springerville, Arizona. The site is one of the very few that link the Mogollon to a modern Pueblo. It is still visited for religious purposes by people from Zuni Pueblo. The Pinedale Black-on-white jar, with stylized butterfly design, the Tularosa Black-on-white "canteen," and the Reserve Black-on-white ladle are all Late Mogollon/ Western Pueblo types. The color schemes and designs resemble Anasazi pottery of the same period.

In his tabulation of subject matter on 733 figurative vessels, Brody comments that considering the actual wealth and variety of species in the Mimbres environment, the number of creatures depicted on the pottery is remarkably limited. Yet, neither the pattern of the selection of creatures or its meaning is clear. Further, there are few hints about either topic in the oral literature of living southwestern people. Certainly some animals that are important in Pueblo oral literature are depicted, but others, just as important, are not. Finally, Brody remarks that neither economic importance, rarity, ubiquity, character, or potential decorative value seems to have been a factor for selecting the figures portrayed. Myth, history, and literature are certainly the factors that were used but may never be known.

Between A.D. 1100 and 1150, the long continuum of occupation of the Mimbres Valley breaks down. LeBlanc attributes the demise of Mimbres culture, in part, to its success. He finds that between A.D. 200 and 1100, the Mimbres population grew and settlement expanded throughout the valley.

Eventually, communities were established on land that was only marginally suited to agriculture. LeBlanc suggests that firewood and game were depleted over time so that when several years of poor rainfall, beginning in A.D. 1150, caused crop failures, there were few backup resources left, and many sites were abandoned.

At about the same time, however, a new center of population was beginning to develop at Casas Grandes in what is today the state of Chihuahua, Mexico. LeBlanc suggests that some Mimbres people may have migrated to Casas Grandes. Those who stayed in the Mimbres Valley were greatly influenced by their newly powerful southern neighbors. For example, cobble masonry was replaced by construction in adobe, the material used at Casas Grandes. Basin-shaped hearths made of adobe replaced the earlier rectangular, slab-lined hearths. About half the burials were cremations interred in jars, a form new to the area. Ceramics also changed dramatically to types with polychrome painted designs and a new series of cooking wares. LeBlanc considers that the coherence and continuity we identify as Mimbres was gone by A.D. 1150. Later developments in the area are related to external events.

The differences between the Mogollon of the Mimbres Valley and those of the Grasshopper and Q Ranch regions are not tremendous. They are differences in size, numbers, and detail. The Mimbres Valley seems to have supported a larger and more sedentary occupation than the two more northerly regions. This, in turn, can be attributed to the greater abundance of good farming land in the Mimbres area. As greater numbers inhabited the Mimbres Valley, the pace of change accelerated. Some of the stylistic differences between the two areas may relate to their geographic distance from each other and their proximity to different neighboring traditions. The Mimbres people are seen as having been influenced more by their southern neighbors at Casas Grandes, while the residents of the Grasshopper Plateau are viewed as having greater interactions with the Anasazi whose territory adjoined theirs to the north.

Change in the Mimbres area is generally described as developing in place, primarily as a result of internal factors. In the Grasshopper region change and diversity in artifact inventories are more often attributed to interactions among diverse ethnic populations. These differences may be no more than disparate views among archaeologists, or they may reflect situations that were truly different. The subregions contrasted here are the most thoroughly studied in Mogollon territory. They nevertheless represent only a small fraction of that part of the Southwest that was Mogollon. With continued study of other subregions, we may be better able to explain the differences between the Mimbres people and the mountain-dwelling Mogollon, or we may find that entirely different scenarios were played out in other locations.

The tower at Square Tower House is the tallest structure at Mesa Verde. Between A.D. 1200 and 1300, Mesa Verdeans built most of their long period of Anasazi occupation of the area—between A.D. 650 and 1200—most dwellings were sited in the open on the mesa tops.

5

THE EMERGENCE OF THE ANASAZI

The first time many Americans heard the name Anasazi or learned anything at all about the ancient ruins of the Southwest was at the Chicago World's Columbian Exposition, which ran from May to October of 1893. There, a gigantic Anthropological Building housed more than 150 exhibits devoted to archaeology and ethnology. Included were collections from Mesa Verde, Colorado, and Grand Gulch, Utah. The Mesa Verde collections had been amassed in 1891-1892 by Richard Wetherill,

homes under rock overhangs. Before then, in the

In the winter of 1888, rancher Richard Wetherill and his friend Charlie Mason were searching for stray cattle when they became the first European-Americans to discover Cliff Palace at Mesa Verde. The Wetherill family is shown here resting among the ruins of Cliff Palace.

In 1879, 22-year-old Frank Hamilton Cushing traveled to the Southwest for the Smithsonian's Bureau of Ethnology to learn about the customs of Native Americans. Cushing spent four years among the Zuni; for him, there was little doubt that the Pueblos were descended from the Anasazi.

The Wetherill family were ranchers in Mancos, Colorado. Richard had learned about the ruins by exploring and digging in them. His interest in, and respect for, the people who had built the cliff dwellings were greatly enhanced when he guided Baron Gustaf Eric Adolf Nordenskjöld, a young Swedish archaeologist, to Mesa Verde in 1891. Nordenskjöld was trained in the techniques of excavation and recording proper for his day, and Wetherill learned much from him. Nordenskjöld's later (1901) publication was the first scholarly description of the ruins of Mesa Verde, and it made his professional reputation.

To the visitors at the Chicago fair, Wetherill described the Anasazi as ancient inhabitants of North America, among the very few about whom there was, at the time, any information at all. The name Anasazi, he explained, was a Navajo word used to refer to the ancient people, then long gone, whose ruined houses were found by the Navajo when they first entered the plateau country of southern Colorado. In a vague way, Wetherill knew that the name referred to ancient enemies, but whether or not this meant that the Navajo had actually encountered and fought with these people he did not know.

The name Anasazi was officially sanctioned by Alfred V. Kidder in 1936 as a less cumbersome alternative to Basketmaker-Pueblo. Neil M. Judd, another of the great first fathers of Southwest archaeology and the excavator of Pueblo Bonito, noted that although the word Anasazi was not included in the 1912 vocabulary of the Navajo language published by the Franciscan Friars, it was well known to all who had worked in Navajo country where ruins of the ancient ones abound.

Neil M. Judd, shown standing in the photograph at right, was one of the foremost archaeologists of the Southwest, and was responsible for the excavation of Pueblo Bonito in Chaco Canyon.

Among early anthropologists, such as William Henry Holmes, Jesse Walter Fewkes, and Frank Hamilton Cushing, who had worked among the Pueblos, there was never any doubt that the Anasazi were ancestral Pueblo. But the vast land along the San Juan River that sheltered ancient Pueblo homes was occupied by Navajo, a people completely different in culture and language from the Pueblos. From the perspective of the ranchers and explorers of southern Colorado and Utah, the ancient ones had vanished. The Navajo knew little about them. It is also likely that most visitors to the Chicago fair, and many among the more than 16 million tourists who have since visited Mesa Verde National Park, did not understand that Navajo and Pueblo peoples are very different, have mistrusted one another, and often have been enemies.

The vast landscape that was once the homeland of the Anasazi centers on the Colorado Plateau, but extends from central New Mexico, on the east, to southern Nevada, on the west. The northern boundary loops through southern Nevada, Utah, and Colorado, while the southern boundary follows the Colorado and Little Colorado rivers in Arizona, and the Rio Puerco to the Rio Grande in New Mexico with extensions eastward toward the Great Plains on the Cimarron and Pecos rivers and the Galisteo Basin. The plateau portion of this region is generally high, with elevations ranging from about 4500 to 8500 feet (1370 to 2600 meters). The mesas are capped by extensive, nearly horizontal sedimentary formations and support pinyon-juniper woodland except at the higher elevations where there are forests of ponderosa and yellow pine. Steep-

The heartland of the Anasazi was the San Juan River drainage, but Anasazi territory eventually extended over much of the Colorado Plateau, and the basin-and-range country of northern New Mexico. Archaeologists divide this territory into a number of subregions, based on variations in pottery design and decoration, and architectural forms.

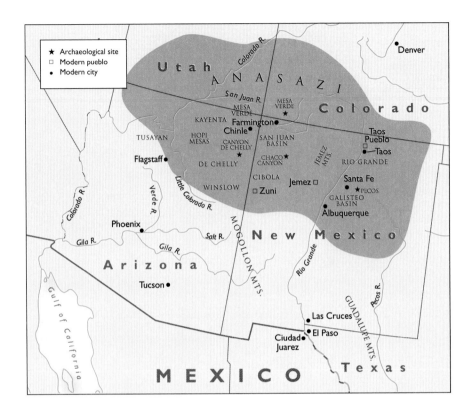

walled canyons and escarpments are common features. Wind erosion has sculpted windows, bridges, and spires out of the sandstone. Where softer sandstone overlies harder sandstone, shales, or limestones, the wind has hollowed out rock overhangs, creating the shelters and caves used by the Anasazi over the centuries. Moisture from the winter snows percolates through the sandstone and accumulates at junctures of sandstone overlying shales, forming seeps and springs that were key sources of household water for the Anasazi.

Other parts of the Anasazi homeland are basin-and-range country similar to that occupied by the Mogollon. The San Juan, Gallup-Zuni, Galisteo, and Albuquerque basins are low, arid, and somewhat featureless landforms supporting desert grasses and shrubs, except along stream-beds where there are willows, reeds, grasses, and dense shrubs. Also within the Anasazi domain are mountains that reach elevations of 12,000 feet (3650 meters). The highest are capped by meadows and draped in great evergreen pine forests. The mountains are the origins of the rivers and streams fed by winter snows. For the Anasazi, the mountains were sources of timber for building, game animals, obsidians and cherts used for flaked tools, and mineral ores used as pigment in paints.

The major rivers of Anasazi country—the San Juan, Little Colorado, Chama, Rio Grande, and Pecos—are relatively great rivers for the arid

This corrugated pot found in Canyon de Chelly clearly shows the Anasazi potters' method: coils of clay were built up one on top of another, pinched together, and scraped on the inside with a shell, gourd, or other object. The corrugations on this vessel were made with vertical finger impressions across the coils. Such vessels were used by the Anasazi as everyday cookware and for storing foods.

This Anasazi Black-on-white mug was found during the excavation of Sand Canyon Pueblo, near Cortez, Colorado. Typically, Anasazi serving vessels were painted with black lines on a white clay background. The mug form as well as the wide black line are typical of the Mesa Verde region.

landscape. They carry heavy silt loads and are deeply entrenched for miles or are subject to flooding. Difficult to tame with the technology available to the Anasazi, they were less important for agriculture than their smaller tributaries, such as the Chinle, Animas, La Plata, Jemez, Santa Fe, and Taos. As with other parts of the Southwest, the accumulation of winter snows provides moisture crucial for germination of seeds in the spring. The amount of snowfall and the duration and intensity of summer thunderstorms vary from year to year and area to area. Anasazi agricultural and social strategies buffered these variations remarkably well. At times, though, there was nothing the Anasazi could do but leave their fields and homes, just as 19th- and 20th-century homesteaders of this region have also had to do when all else failed.

Although not quite as large as the Mogollon region, the Anasazi area is large enough so that developments did not proceed at a uniform pace across its entirety, and there were stylistic and other differences from one location to another. As with the Mogollon, archaeologists divide the Anasazi area into named subregions. From west to east, these are the Virgin, Kayenta, Tusayan, De Chelly, and Winslow (or Middle Little Colorado), Northern San Juan,

Cibola (or Chaco), and Rio Grande. The names do not imply a single political structure, language, or ethnic derivation, however. Rather, they refer to geographically circumscribed subregions within which ceramic technology, ceramic design styles, and architectural forms are distinctive and relatively homogeneous. The rate of change is also internally consistent.

The most general framework used for the entire Anasazi region is the Pecos Classification, originally proposed in 1927 as one outcome of the first Pecos Conference and published later that year by A. V. Kidder in *Science* magazine. Although the classifications were not initially tied to calendar dates, the development of tree-ring dating overcame that particular difficulty. Nevertheless, as the dendrochronology dates began to accumulate from excavations throughout the region, it became obvious that change had not occurred at a uniform rate. In a summary written in 1940 for the Smithsonian Institution, Neil Judd remarked that the most illuminating fact to have emerged from what he termed an avalanche of fieldwork was the discovery that Pueblo culture had advanced rapidly but without uniformity, so that there was no smooth and regular progress as had been proposed by the Pecos scheme.

The Anasazi sequence began, as had the Mogollon, when pottery was added to a way of life based on a mixed economy of maize agriculture and gathering and hunting, which had developed as a continuation of the local San Jose Archaic. Over much of the Anasazi area, pottery occurs at about A.D. 200 to 300, but is not abundant until about A.D. 500, or the Basketmaker III period according to the Pecos Classification. The pottery of the later date is gray in color. Cooking ware was undecorated, but serving vessels were decorated with black painted designs on an unslipped, gray background. By the 6th century, the Anasazi were living in shallow pithouses in communities of variable size. Small, basally notched projectile points replaced the larger, side-notched Archaic points, indicating a change from the spear-thrower to the bow and arrow. Beans were added to the list of crops at this time. Basketmaker III burials reveal long-headed (when measured from front to back) individuals of medium stature. Skulls were not artificially deformed. By contrast, from about A.D. 700 to historic times, the Anasazi flattened the backs of their skulls by using hard cradleboards for infants. Cradleboards, like swaddling, are used to keep babies safe and out of trouble. Since it matters little for the child's safety whether or not the back of the board is padded, the hard board was presumably used to achieve what must have been considered an aesthetically pleasing result.

Between A.D. 700 and 900, Pueblo I in the Pecos scheme, there was a major change in Anasazi housing. In the early part of the period, sites consist of long arcs of *jacal* (pole-and-mud) surface storage rooms placed behind a squarish pithouse. Somewhat later, hearths and domestic debris indicate that the surface rooms were used as living rooms. Pithouses were retained, however, and were used either as kivas or, during the coldest months, as dwellings. The pithouses

The arid canyons of what is now southern Utah represented the northern limits of Anasazi settlement. However, some canyon bottoms have little fertile soil, making agriculture difficult at the best of times; locally gathered wild foods were used to supplement crops of corn, beans, and squash. By 1250, the Anasazi had abandoned this uncompromising region. This site lies in what is now Canyonlands National Park.

may have served both functions. Culinary pottery has unobliterated coils at the vessel neck, a treatment called neck banding. In addition to black-on-white painted pottery, red-on-orange and black-on-red types were produced. This also is the first period during which cranial flattening was practiced.

Pueblo II, dated between 900 and 1150, was a time of marked dispersal and regional differentiation among the Anasazi. During this period, the events in Chaco Canyon changed course abruptly and eventually had tremendous influence on the entire San Juan River and adjacent mountains. The characteristics of the Chaco region are discussed in detail in Chapter 6. It is certain, however, that Chaco influenced the Anasazi of neighboring areas.

Outside Chaco Canyon and the San Juan Basin, Pueblo II was a time when sites were somewhat smaller and more dispersed than before. Pueblo II cooking pottery has exterior corrugations, and painted wares are predominantly black-on-white with designs in a variety of regional styles. During this time, surface architecture was constructed more regularly of masonry and became primarily residential. The pithouse with elaborated features was retained as a communal structure, or kiva.

Pueblo III dates from 1150 to 1300. In the Pecos Classification, Pueblo III is traditionally described in developmental terms as Great Pueblo. It was a time of little innovation but great refinement in Pueblo skills and crafts. Domestic architecture consisted of multistory pueblos constructed with well-shaped masonry. Kiva architecture was also elaborated in some areas, with tower kivas and great kivas incorporating specialized floor features. Also noticeably refined and executed were the designs on black-on-white pottery. Then, in A.D. 1130, a severe drought affected the region. Some Anasazi areas were abandoned, and the population pulled in to a shrinking core area. The system that had been developing and operating in Chaco Canyon from A.D. 900 ceased to function as it had. Chaco was not actually abandoned at this time, but the character of its occupation changed and its influence greatly diminished.

After 1150, the population of areas around Chaco Canyon, such as Mesa Verde, Canyon de Chelly, and Zuni, grew rapidly, and large, aggregated settlements were constructed. By 1300, the entire northern tier of the Anasazi world had been abandoned. There were no longer Anasazi living in what is now southern Nevada, Utah, or Colorado. Attempts to explain an event of this magnitude have occupied archaeologists for nearly a century. With the abandonment of so much of the Anasazi region, Pueblo IV witnessed a population increase in the Chama and Rio Grande regions, at Zuni, and in the Little Colorado region and the Hopi mesas. At this time, too, the Mogollon region was dominated by events at Casas Grandes in Chihuahua. (The dynamics of social and ideological change during this period are discussed in detail in Chapters 7 and 8.) Nevertheless, while communities in much of the Anasazi world vanished, the people themselves, together with their skills, ideas, and beliefs, moved into the then thinly occupied territories where their descendants continue to live successfully to the present day.

In 1927, when the Pecos Classification was codified, the Four Corners region and the Northern San Juan drainage—the country explored so diligently by Richard Wetherill, his patrons, and friends—was known in more detail than any other part of the Southwest. The classification works far better within the Four Corners region than it does elsewhere, as is to be expected. In the last 65 years, a great deal has been learned about the Anasazi of the Four Corners and the Anasazi of other settings. The avalanche of data to which Neil Judd referred in 1940 must seem like an anthill beside the information that has been accumulating ever since. The development of the Anasazi regional tradition will be explored in more detail for two areas: the Northern San Juan Basin and immediately adjacent localities, on which the original classification focused, and the Kayenta area to the west, which provides unique details and perspectives on the variety in Anasazi society.

The Northern San Juan has long been considered the wellspring of Anasazi culture. In excavations carried out between 1956 and 1968 in conjunction with construction of the Navajo Reservoir, archaeologists A. E. Dittert and Frank Eddy surprised their fellow southwesternists by discovering Basketmaker sites that dated from about A.D. 200 to 700 (equivalent to Basketmaker II and III in other parts of the San Juan). They found a brown pottery ware and both surface dwellings and shallow pithouses. Brown ware has long been thought to be a hallmark of Mogollon culture. The received wisdom was that the difference between Mogollon brown ware and Anasazi gray ware was a question of the technique used in firing. Brown wares were fired in an oxidizing atmosphere, where the air is allowed to circulate openly, whereas gray wares were fired in a reducing atmosphere, from which air is blocked. Since the late 1960s, brown ware has been reported from Basketmaker sites in the Northern San Juan region, but its occurrence is rare. The pottery itself is very friable, and the sites where it exists are often obscured by later occupations.

Two discoveries, reported in the early 1990s, have shed some light on the appearance and nature of this early northern brown ware. Studies by Dean C. Wilson, a ceramic specialist at the Museum of New Mexico, have demonstrated that the brown ware comes from the use of iron-rich alluvial clays. The earliest Mogollon and the earliest Anasazi pottery were brown wares made of this kind of clay. The clay seems to have been used when people were farming the alluvial clay bottomlands, possibly when neither their social network nor the annual patterns of movement included areas where there were better-quality geologic clays. The second recent finding is that in the northern San Juan area, if not elsewhere as well, the sites with this earliest occurrence of pottery-making among the Anasazi are virtually invisible from the surface. They are either buried under later occupations or beneath quantities of alluvium. Both conditions led to their having been overlooked in the field and markedly underrepresented in the literature.

By A.D. 550 to 650, Basketmaker III communities were well established across most of the Colorado Plateau. The typical Basketmaker III house was a shallow pithouse, round—or square with rounded corners—with an antechamber and fairly consistent floor features. These include a central hearth, ash pits, often mud dividers or wing walls that separate activity space inside the dwelling, and some interior storage cists. Within this general pattern, there are a number of regional variations. In the Kayenta area, and the San Juan Basin, pithouse walls are often lined with upright slabs. In the Kayenta region, storage pits are consistently located behind the pithouses. In the Mesa Verde region, one excavation—the Gilliland Site—consisted of four pithouses and numerous outside work areas with *ramadas* (shade structures), completely encircled by a stockade. In the Mesa Verde region, pithouse entryways are oriented to the south. In Chaco, the entryways point to the southeast, and there are many other minor differences as well.

Basketmaker communities vary considerably in size, but it is not always clear how many people lived in them at the same time, nor how sedentary the Basketmaker way of life really was. For example, Shabik'eschee Village, situated on one of several small mesas that protrude above the south side of Chaco Canyon, has long been considered typical of Basketmaker III settlements. Frank H. H. Roberts, Jr., originally and meticulously excavated Shabik'eschee in 1926 and 1927. He found 18 pithouses, more than 48 exterior storage pits, and one oversize structure regarded as a great kiva. Shabik'eschee is most often discussed by archaeologists because it has been excavated and carefully studied, not because it is unique. Sites of similar size and age cover the tops of the small mesas fingering into the canyon above Chaco Wash. Recent surveys have recorded at least 163 such settlements at Chaco Canyon alone. If all these sites and all their pithouses were occupied at one time, then 16,000 people—an absurdly high figure—would have lived there. Roberts, in fact, recognized two distinct periods of occupation at Shabik'eschee based on the stratigraphy of the structures.

Archaeologists Wirt H. Wills and Thomas C. Windes have recently reevaluated Shabik'eschee, based on a review of the original field notes and subsequent work. They argue that Shabik'eschee represents one kind of Basketmaker III settlement strategy. The strategy involved a small resident core population—perhaps one or two families—and periodic use by a larger group. Wills and Windes maintain that the larger group would have been attracted to the site at times when there was an unusual abundance of resources. The basic Basketmaker strategy, they conclude, would be one of small, seasonally occupied camps.

What seems to be another, highly unusual, example of Basketmaker response to local abundance has been reported for the Upper San Juan by archaeologist Nancy Hammack. A site known as L.A. 4169 consisted of two compact clusters of burned pits that had been excavated from a clay ridge above the present shore of the Navajo Reservoir. Part of the site had been excavated by Dittert and Eddy in 1962-63, the rest in 1987. The pits themselves were quite well preserved, because they had been dug out of massive silty clay and then burned. Thus, they became what Hammack calls in-place terra-cotta storage jars.

Fired clay features such as these are amenable to archaeomagnetic dating, and samples were taken from five pits. The results indicated not only that the pits belonged to Basketmaker III times (A.D. 600), but that, in all likelihood, the five had been fired at roughly the same time. Given their size—a volume of 5.0 cubic meters—and the admittedly extreme assumption that all the pits had been used at the same time, Hammack estimates a total of 110.5 cubic meters of stored food. Using commonly applied figures based on maize, she finds that the storage capacity of the site would have fed at least 138 persons, or 27 families, for a period of one year! As was suggested for Shabik'eschee, there appear to have been times when a great abundance of a particular food resource encouraged large population aggregates, at least temporarily. We do not know how frequently these local abundances occurred; probably they were unusual, and the overall poverty of southwestern environments certainly supports this view. Still, the estimated storage

Basketmaker pithouse dwellings were usually sunk a few feet into the ground. Four main timbers at the corners supported the roof, which was made of mud laid on branches over a wooden framework. The example shown above is a reconstruction at Mesa Verde.

capacity at L.A. 4169 gives one pause when we remember that the early Anasazi led difficult and impoverished lives.

Painted Basketmaker III ceramics mark the beginning of two different conventions in the manufacture of black paint. One was preparing black paint by using a mineral—usually iron oxide—as pigment, in some kind of flux. The use of mineral-based paints centered in northwestern New Mexico, especially in the San Juan Basin, and extended east to the Rio Grande and south to Mogollon country. West of this, in the Kayenta area and farther west, a carbon-based black pigment was produced from vegetal materials—most commonly, the Rocky Mountain bee plant. The two traditions coexisted until potters in the central Anasazi area, the San Juan Basin, Mesa Verde, and the Chuska drainage switched to carbon pigments. This occurred gradually between about 1050 and 1200. South of these areas, from the Rio Puerco east to the edge of the Great Plains, mineral paints were retained until nearly historic times. Initially, the painted pottery of both traditions was much the same: a pattern of simple lines, apparently derived from basketry patterns decorating the interior of bowls.

Basketmaker III seems to have been a time in which much of what we see as Anasazi for the next 700 years crystallizes over the Colorado Plateau. This pattern includes the cultivation of corn, beans, and squash; the use of plain gray cooking ware and black-on-white serving and storage vessels; and the use of the bow and arrow. Although surface pueblos replaced pithouses as dwellings, the use of semisubterranean rooms continues in the pueblo pattern as communal rooms and kivas. Even in rock art there is a Pueblo style that is first seen in Basketmaker III. It consists of strongly pecked elements that include stick figures with rectangular bodies and small heads, and the depiction of a flute player who is represented in a variety of human, animal, and insect forms, both with and without a humpback. Other elements in this style are human hand- and footprints and animal tracks. The rock art is produced on cliff and rock faces, often in panel groupings.

In traditional Hopi legend, there is a hump-backed flute player, named Kokopelli. As part of traditional Pueblo religious ritual, altars are set up displaying panels which depict images of great symbolic importance. Some figures in Basketmaker III rock art appear to be masked, and masking is another significant element in Pueblo rituals. The combination of economic, organizational, and ideological elements that are so obviously essentially Pueblo led scholars to view Basketmaker III as an emergent Pueblo culture. It is also worth acknowledging that we do not know what these symbols meant in Basketmaker society or whether or not the elements that we regard as interrelated correspond to Basketmaker behavior and beliefs. Further, in part because many Basketmaker III pithouse settlements were apparently occupied on a seasonal basis, the mobility that was part of the Basketmaker III economic strategy implies a set of community and regional relationships that were quite different from those of later, sedentary Pueblos.

A pictograph on volcanic rock from the Galisteo Basin, New Mexico, at the eastern edge of Anasazi territory, shows a flute player and a shield, suggesting Kokopelli, the hump-backed flute player who figures in traditional Hopi folklore today.

Pictographs showing masked, human-like figures have been found at a number of Basketmaker II and III sites in the San Juan River area. The one shown above, known as the Green Mask, is near Grand Gulch, Utah.

The configuration of settlements in the Anasazi area changes between about A.D. 750 and 850 . The Pueblo 1 villages of this period consist of long, arced rows of contiguous surface rooms with a deep, squarish pithouse placed to the south, or in front of the surface rooms. The surface rooms are generally of jacal construction, rather than masonry, but serve as both storage and residential areas. Back rooms that lack floor features, especially hearths, most likely were used for storage. Openings connect these to front rooms with hearths. These, in turn, may open on a portico or outside work area, often also with hearths.

Some Pueblo 1 settlements are very large by any standard. The quintessential grandfather of all Pueblo 1 sites was excavated in 1932 at Alkali Ridge, in southern Utah, by J. O. Brew of Harvard's Peabody Museum. Alkali Ridge Site 13 consisted of 130 surface rooms, 16 pithouses, and 2 kivas. Site 13 is not unique. Sites that are similar in size have been recorded in several locations in southwestern Colorado and southeastern Utah. In general, these sites are located in the relatively well-watered, northern tier of Anasazi settlement.

Recent excavations and reevaluation of older work have shown that most Pueblo 1 sites were occupied a mere 30 years or less. The rather brief duration of these settlements has permitted archaeologists to estimate their population more easily than those of other sites. These estimates indicate larger populations than one might suppose. Using conservative techniques, the estimates indicate that some of these sites housed up to 600 individuals in three separate but closely spaced settlement clusters. The sheer size of the settlement suggests that social mechanisms were already in place, capable of reducing potential conflicts between individuals and families. The large number of people, even if they were only together for 30 years, suggests that Pueblo I settlements had the ability to integrate individuals from several different households in a social context and to maintain that integration for longer than a human generation.

Archaeologist Timothy A. Kohler has worked extensively with Pueblo I sites in the course of a multiyear excavation project near Dolores, Colorado. Kohler observed that the large Pueblo I sites near Dolores were founded when rainfall conditions were particularly good for crops grown without benefit of irrigation. At the same time, areas both to the west and in general at lower elevations, were not experiencing moisture patterns favorable for dry farming. As a result, some of those areas of low elevation were abandoned at this time, possibly as people moved to higher settings. In the more arid western portion of the Colorado Plateau, settlements remained small.

Questions about why and how populations congregate are central ones in archaeology, just as they are in anthropology, geography, and certain fields of biology. Kohler argues that the centralization of population into large settlements creates difficulties for farmers. Some, if not most, fields will be farther away from living areas, obliging farmers to spend time walking to and from their fields and to carry harvested crops greater distances than would be the case if households were located next to their own fields. There must then have been some perceived advantage in forming large settlements. Kohler suggests that one advantage of Pueblo I aggregation was that it facilitated the sharing of agricultural food among community members. At the same time, because only members of the same community were tightly integrated socially, limits could be placed on the extent of the food-sharing network. In those low elevation subregions where dry farming was more tenuous, individual households may have been able to move to new locations in the face of an agricultural failure.

Within localities such as Mesa Verde, some archaeologists argue that the clusters of Pueblo I villages represent the largest population reached prehistorically. Others suggest that although Pueblo I villages do tend to occur in clusters, not all clusters of villages were occupied at the same time. Nevertheless, Pueblo I seems to represent one aspect of a longer-term Anasazi pattern. Simply stated, there were times when larger populations could be supported, but they were not long-lasting. There was an oscillation between coming together and dispersal that, when seen at a different scale, becomes an oscillation between occupation and abandonment. If dispersed populations gather in one place, then most of the land they once occupied is abandoned unless someone else moves in. From the perspective of one area, the cycles become what archaeologists William Lipe and R. G. Matson refer to as boom and bust. The instability of congregated populations derives from one of two factors: either the inability of the southwestern environment to support them over a substantial period or the failure of mechanisms of social integration to keep people together.

We do not know how the Pueblo I aggregates were organized socially. Throughout the plateaus where populations were somewhat dispersed, there are great kivas that may have integrated several settlements. At the big, aggregated Pueblo I settlements, very large pit structures with unusual floor features may have served a similar function.

Certain general features and symbols seem to have integrated much of the Anasazi area during Pueblo I. Black-on-white ceramics share a design style, called Kana-a or Red Mesa, that is strikingly similar throughout the region, even though the pottery was made locally and might differ in technological details, such as type of pigment. Items of trade included marine shells, shell artifacts, and pottery. The trade pottery is generally San Juan red ware. This includes types made in southern Utah and traded out to the Mesa Verde, Chaco, and Kayenta areas. These red wares do not make up substantial percentages of decorated ceramics in the regions into which they were traded, but they do demonstrate information flow throughout very large parts of Pueblo territory.

Between about A.D. 900 and 1150, the Anasazi reached their greatest territorial extent. At the same time, places like Mesa Verde experienced a slight population decline. Pueblo communities were smaller than they had been in Pueblo I, but they were greatly dispersed over the landscape. In the western Anasazi region, peoples of the Kayenta Anasazi tradition expanded north of the San Juan and west to the Grand Canyon and the Virgin River area of southern Nevada. As archaeologists George Gumerman and Jeffrey Dean have noted for the main Kayenta area, Pueblo II habitation sites occupied "virtually every conceivable spot," avoiding only floodplains during times when they were buried by streams which deposited quantities of sediment on them.

At Mesa Verde, Pueblo II settlements were dispersed on all the locally available topographic situations (mesa tops, talus slopes, canyon bottoms, and side canyons). This dispersal is associated with the first indications of methods used to enhance agricultural production. These are soil and water-control features such as check dams, terraces, and linear borders.

For the Kayenta area, Gumerman and Dean note that the only real change in material culture at this time is a decrease in the quantity, and particularly the quality, of stone projectile points. This reflects, they suggest, the diminished importance of the larger game animals since population expansion probably depleted the game supply. At Mesa Verde, excavated rooms containing turkey dung and egg shell indicate that turkeys were either domesticated or tamed and kept at about this time, potentially confirming an important solution to declining game supplies.

Mesa Verde kivas are generally keyhole shaped, and often include a low, narrow bench and pilasters. The kiva floor usually has a hearth or firebox, a deflector, and a ventilator. Most also have a small round hole in the floor. This is called a *sipapu* by the modern Pueblos, who believe that it represents the place where humans came up from the underworld.

During the same period, sites become very standardized in appearance. Domestic sites consist of a block of masonry habitation and storage rooms generally arranged in an east-west line, L-shape, or short arc. In front of these rooms, in a north-south line, are a midden and a kiva. This pattern was described as a "unit pueblo" by T. Mitchell Prudden in 1903. Today archaeologists often refer to these sites as Prudden Unit Pueblos. Gumerman and Dean note that these sites rarely contain more than 12 rooms. Such sites could hardly have accommodated more than a moderately large extended family. Nevertheless, they appear quite self-contained and economically independent. On the other hand, archaeologist Arthur Rohn has commented that for the Mesa Verde and Northern San Juan in general, such unit pueblos could not have been functioning communities in any real sense. Although they are treated as separate sites by archaeologists, Rohn comments that they do form some spatial clustering on the landscape. The larger spatial clusters are more likely communities of day-to-day interaction.

For the western Anasazi area, Gumerman and Dean observe that although the early years of Pueblo II saw a considerable exchange in raw materials for stone tools and finished products, an increasing use of local resources becomes dominant by A.D. 1000. By that date, there are highly specific local traditions in ceramics and architectural forms. Some of the architectural specialization extends to the Northern San Juan region, where it is reflected particularly in kiva architecture. For example, Mesa Verde kivas are known for their stone pilasters and for assuming, eventually, a keyhole shape. In the San Juan Basin, kivas are generally round with an interior encircling bench. Common kiva floor features include a hearth or firebox, a deflector, and a ventilator. A small hole in the floor is referred to as a *sipapu* by archaeologists because this is the term used for them in modern pueblos, where they represent the *shipap*, the place where humans emerged from the underworld.

As people began to inhabit surface rooms and use the pit structure more for communal and, probably, ritual functions, and as the form of pit structures was modified and standardized, it is appropriate to use the term "kiva" and to consider that these structures likely did serve functions similar to those in modern Pueblo villages. The forms of kivas and their various floor features demonstrate continuity over centuries in this aspect of architecture. We cannot, however, be certain that various forms of ritual or even the use of kivas by specific groups of people, such as adult males, is of similar antiquity.

At the same time that much of the Anasazi area was looking inward and becoming provincial in terms of decreased exchange and interaction, the communities in Chaco Canyon and the San Juan Basin were expanding and becoming the first regionally organized system in the Pueblo homeland. As we have seen, the Chaco system developed during a period when rainfall was quite good, or at least adequate for corn, and farmers should have prospered. Perhaps it was the relatively benign climate, as a background, that enabled the rest of the Pueblo II world to remain self-contained and self-sufficient. If so, this climatic background was so forgiving as to allow virtually any settlement and economic strategies to work. Success, however, may well have been the seed of eventual decline. As Anasazi farmers extended their communities and fields to increasingly peripheral areas, they depleted the available supplies of game, firewood, and probably some wild plant foods as well. Poor soil and inadequate growing conditions made many of the peripheral areas marginal for the cultivation of corn. When conditions reverted to their difficult "normal" state of aridity, or with the onset of the drought of 1130, those communities on the most distant edges of the Anasazi realm, and those closer in but inhabiting poor farmland, were the first to be abandoned and left in ruins.

Chaco Canyon, seen here from the air, seems an unlikely place for a culture to take root and flourish, but a thousand years ago this arid valley between A.D. 900 and 1150, the Anasazi built 14 pueblo great houses here. Pueblo Bonito, the largest of these, can be seen nestling beneath

was a major center of Anasazi life. In the period
the cliffs.

6

NETWORKS FROM CHACO CANYON

Today, one can drive into Chaco Canyon by way of Crown Point, Farmington, or Nageezi, New Mexico. The trip is not terribly long. But in winter, the roads may be snow-covered and icy. In spring they are often streams of mud; by summer, dry and rutted, or—if there has been a thunderstorm—slick and oily. But at any time of the year it can feel like a drive to the end of the earth. One of Chaco's essential qualities is the feeling of being in the middle of nowhere. Visitors to the cool, wooded mesa tops and sheltered side canyons of Mesa Verde admire the cliff dwellings and wonder why the Anasazi abandoned them. In Chaco Canyon, however, the question is what brought the Anasazi here in the first place.

The name Chaco means desert in a regional Spanish dialect. In 1924, A. V. Kidder described Chaco Canyon as such, writing, "the district is little better than a desert: many parts of it, indeed, are absolutely barren wastes of sand and rock which do not even support the usual dry-country flora of the Southwest." Archaeologist R. Gwinn Vivian, author of the most substantive study of Chaco Canyon prehistory, reminds us that Chaco looks better now than it did in Kidder's time because grazing has been controlled. Chaco Canyon is, nonetheless, a small slash in the relatively featureless, barren, and dry San Juan Basin.

The geologic basin covers some 26,000 square miles (67,350 square kilometers), mostly in New Mexico, but extending into Arizona, Utah, and Colorado. The basin is drained by Chaco Wash, the San Juan and Zuni rivers, the Rio Puerco on the east, and the Chaco River on the west. The rivers originate in the highland areas surrounding the basin, while the basin itself is characterized by its overall aridity. During the last several decades, annual precipitation in Chaco Canyon has averaged about 8.5 inches (21 centimeters). Averages are misleading, however, because there is great variation from one year to another. For example, over a three-year period in the 1970s, annual precipitation in Chaco Canyon ranged between 7.3 and 13.7 inches (18.5 and 34.7 centimeters), numbers that tightly bracket the 12 to 14 inches (30 to 35 centimeters) required to grow corn successfully. Finally, although the amount and timing of precipitation are the most important factors in the success or failure of maize agriculture in the basin, there is the potential for damaging early and late frosts.

Despite the bleakness of the landscape, the aridity, and the vagaries of necessary rain, Chaco Canyon contains some of the most abundant and impressive prehistoric architectural remains in the United States. Between about A.D. 900 and 1150, the Anasazi of Chaco built 14 magnificent pueblo great houses in Chaco Canyon. Over the same period, they built and remodeled scores of small village settlements in the canyon. The sandstone architecture of the Chacoan great houses is visually spectacular, a silent tribute to the skills and aesthetics of the Anasazi. More impressive, however, is the fact that at least 200,000 timbers were used in this construction and that these represent, almost entirely, trees that do not now grow, and could not at the time have grown, closer than 40 to 50 miles (65 to 80 kilometers) from the canyon. The carefully dressed stone masonry of Chaco Canyon is testimony to Anasazi planning and fine craftsmanship. The huge number of imported beams is evidence of a remarkable ability to organize human labor.

The abundant wood used in construction at Chaco provides archaeologists with an unusually precise tree-ring chronology for ordering the general

The 14 large towns (*right*) of Chaco Canyon, which today forms part of Chaco Culture National Historical Park, were the nucleus of a wide network that extended far to the north, south, and west (*below*), and embraced communities known as outliers. Recent research suggests the Chacoan road system may have been more extensive than shown below. The extreme variability of rainfall in this region made human habitation difficult.

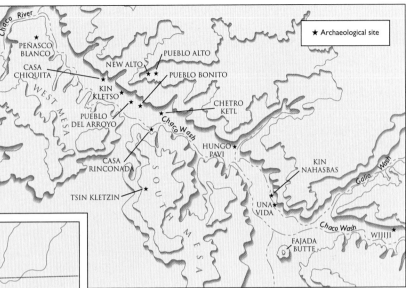

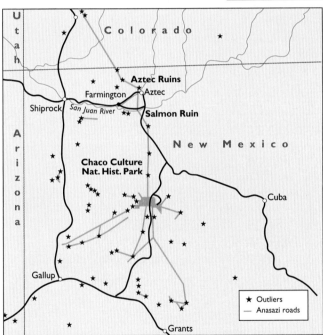

sequence of prehistoric events. The chronological framework used for Chaco divides the sequence during which most construction took place into phases named for the canyon's largest and best-known site, Pueblo Bonito. The Early Bonito phase dates from about A.D. 850 to 1000. During this period construction of the first multistory great houses took place. This period of building is associated with a mineral paint pottery type called Red Mesa Black-on-white, after the Red Mesa Valley, south of Chaco Canyon.

The second phase, or Classic Bonito period, began in about A.D. 1000 and lasted until about A.D. 1100. It was a period during which older structures were enlarged and new great houses were built. There was also a major effort devoted to the construction of great kivas—18 of these enormous features were built during this time. Red Mesa Black-on-white pottery continued to be prevalent, but a new pottery type, Gallup Black-on-white, was added.

A Late Bonito or McElmo phase (named after the McElmo wash, or drainage), between A.D. 1100 and 1150, witnessed changes in both building style and ceramic types. McElmo great houses are more compact than their predecessors, and the masonry style that characterizes them resembles stonework of the northern San Juan and Mesa Verde areas. Pottery also shows a northern affinity. The distinguishing type is carbon black painted Chaco-McElmo Black-on-white. Between about 1200 and 1300, the few

Chaco olla

Chaco pitcher

Chaco-McElmo Black-on-white

Gallup Black-on-white

Reserve Black-on-white

Red Mesa Black-on-white

Classic Anasazi pottery is characterized by fine hatching, and the use of mineral-based paint on a chalky white background. Tall cylindrical shapes were used for some ceremonial vessels. Narrow-necked jars, called ollas, may have been used for liquids. After A.D. 1130-1150, the Chaco-McElmo, Gallup, Red Mesa, Puerco, and Reserve Black-on-white styles have much in common with types made in the northern San Juan and Mesa Verde regions, especially in heavier black-line decoration and the use of carbon-based paint.

Anasazi who remained in Chaco Canyon were most closely affiliated with the northern San Juan. By 1300, Chaco Canyon was deserted. Winter snow and rain weakened roof timbers until, ignored, they collapsed. Sand and dust then accumulated in the open rooms.

The development of Classic Bonito-phase architecture and building took centuries. Over this time, sites in the canyon also became central to an organization of regional scale. There are five characteristics that archaeologists use to define and recognize the distinctive stamp of Chaco Canyon and its regional network: the presence of two different kinds of settlements, called great houses and villages, both built and used at the same time in Chaco Canyon itself; Chacoan outlier communities throughout the San Juan Basin; prehistoric roadways associated with both outliers and canyon settlements; evidence of agricultural intensification in the canyon; and objects that indicate widespread exchange, interaction, and, perhaps, some specialized production of craft items.

The term "Chacoan great house" is used to refer to pueblos that are architecturally distinctive of the Classic Bonito phase. The great houses themselves are large—those in the canyon average more than 200 rooms. Room size is also substantial and ceilings are high by Anasazi standards. These great houses are formal and were planned in such a way that major architectural units were built at one time. They are oriented to the south, with plaza areas almost always enclosed by a room block or a high wall. C-, D-, or E-shaped, the great houses are predominantly multistory constructions, some with sections that were four to five stories high. In the completed buildings, lower, single-story front rooms faced directly on the plaza. The room blocks were then terraced so that the four- or five-story sections composed the rear of the pueblo. A very common arrangement of interior space is the suite, a series of rooms in a direct line from front to back linked by doorways. In such room suites, the front rooms are larger than back rooms that are thought to have served a storage function. Common architectural details include T-shaped doorways and stone lintels.

Great house wall construction is most often of cored, veneered masonry in which the load-bearing wall core is made of rough, flat stones set in ample mortar, each stone oriented to only one face of the wall and overlapping or abutting the stone on the reverse face, thus creating a structurally sound wall. The wall core was then covered on both sides with courses of sandstone facing, often in alternating bands of thick and thin stones. Though strikingly decorative from a European-American perspective, the veneers served a practical function in slowing the weathering and deterioration of the walls. While the building was in use, these veneers were covered by adobe plaster or matting, or both. Sandstone appropriate for veneer was abundantly available in the cliffs on the north side of the canyon where most of the great houses were built. Nevertheless, with an estimated one

In typical Chaco construction, irregular blocks of sandstone—seen in the wall from Chetro Ketl Ruin at far right—formed the core of walls, which were then covered with thin sandstone veneer. The smoothness of the veneer is evident in the wall at right, from Pueblo Bonito. More than one million pieces of dressed stone are estimated to have gone into Pueblo Bonito alone. Although the veneers are aesthetically appealing to us, they were in fact usually plastered over with mud.

million-plus hand-dressed pieces of sandstone in one building alone, a considerable amount of labor was expended.

Small kivas in the great houses occur in a ratio of 1 to every 29 rooms. In addition to these, however, Chacoan great houses have at least one great kiva incorporated within the plaza area. These Chacoan great kivas are large, of course, measuring up to 63 feet (19.2 meters) in diameter. They also have characteristic features that include square, raised fireboxes, paired masonry "vaults," and four roof supports of either masonry or massive timbers seated on huge, shaped sandstone disks. The function of the "vaults" is not known. One suggestion—among many—is that they were covered with boards and used as foot drums, while another has them filled with earth and used as planting boxes for beans, similar to the present-day Pueblo practice of using kivas to force germination of bean plants. Typically, a low masonry bench encircled the kiva, and entry was obtained either through a recessed masonry stairway or by ladder through a hatchway in the roof. Antechambers and small wall niches are also commonly associated with great kivas. The wall niches at the excavated great kiva in the great house called Chetro Ketl were sealed with masonry. When opened, they were found to contain strings of stone and shell beads and pendants. In addition to great kivas, some Chacoan great houses have circular tower kivas that are two or more stories high. These are most often incorporated in room blocks, with rubble filling the spaces between the round kiva wall and the rectangular room corners.

At the same time (A.D. 850 to 1050) that the great houses were constructed, the Anasazi of Chaco Canyon also built single-story pueblos resembling the Pueblo II settlements found throughout the Anasazi area. These village sites are far more numerous than are the great houses. They are relatively small, averaging 20 to 40 rooms, lack veneer masonry, and seem to have been constructed haphazardly over time, with rooms being added as needed. Village

Pueblo Bonito has yielded many treasures, including a turquoise-encrusted cylinder—a reconstruction of the original object—and an authentic, small, carved jet frog with eyes and collar of turquoise.

sites have only small kivas; however, a separate great kiva, such as the one at the site called Casa Rinconada, may have served several villages.

Both villages and great houses have essentially the same kind of material culture at this time, including Red Mesa and Gallup Black-on-white painted pottery types and corrugated gray cooking ware. Nevertheless, there are differences. Great houses yield more imported luxury items than do the villages. These include finished turquoise and shell jewelry, cylindrical vase-shaped jars, copper bells, and macaw skeletons. However, turquoise fragments and evidence of turquoise manufacture have also been found in the villages.

Another difference between villages and great houses concerns a long-standing mystery about burials. Excavated villages have yielded burials in numbers consistent with those at other Anasazi sites. Great houses, however, are a different matter. When they are excavated, very few burials are encountered. The great houses may contain 250 to 800 rooms and an occupation that spans 200 years, yet the number of burials associated with any one of them can be as low as 20 individuals. If the rooms were occupied in the normal fashion of an estimated two people per ground floor room, then the number of burials is absurdly small. Virtually every archaeological expedition to Chaco Canyon has spent fruitless time searching for the "missing" burials. Some archaeologists cite their absence in support of the idea that these structures were a form of public architecture rather than normal residences.

Gwinn Vivian has made a detailed study comparing Chacoan great houses and villages. In addition to enumerating the contrasts in architecture and material culture, he linked these observations to the fact that in Chaco Canyon itself, great houses are located either on the north side of the canyon or on the mesa tops. The many village sites were built on mesa tops and on both the north and south sides of the canyon. Vivian's fieldwork located a set of features that were part of an unusual method of irrigating fields. He proposed that because Chaco Wash is ephemeral and entrenched, it was not tapped to provide water for fields. Rather, irrigation water was derived from sheet wash as it poured off the mesa top. The water was slowed down and channeled through a series of head gates to bordered grid gardens below, then drained off into Chaco Wash. Summer thunderstorms produced the sheet wash necessary to provide enough irrigation water, but only on the north side of the canyon where the broad, sloping, slick rock mesa top serves as a catchment area for rain. This form of irrigation, though requiring a major investment of labor—particularly during the growing season—allowed the Chacoans to produce a food surplus. Vivian maintained that, as a direct result of their irrigation technology, the great houses, located on the north side of the canyon, developed features of social organization that were different from and more elaborate than those reflected by the village sites.

Attempting to explain the presence of two different, but contemporary, kinds of buildings in Chaco Canyon, as Vivian has tried to do, constitutes a

The great kiva at Casa Rinconada, built in about A.D. 1100, duplicates the great kivas enclosed in the central plazas of such great houses as Pueblo Bonito and Chetro Ketl. Like them, it has a raised firebox, paired masonry "vaults," a low bench, wall niches, a subfloor passage, and an associated antechamber. Casa Rinconada, however, was built on slightly elevated land away from any great house structures. It is thought that such "isolated" great kivas served as gathering places for small villages in their vicinity.

fascinating archaeological challenge. In fact, however, this is only about half the story, because Chaco Canyon was also the focal point of a huge region encompassing the entire San Juan Basin, throughout which both great houses and villages are among the identifying features. Discoveries made in the 1970s established that knowledge of the greater region is absolutely pivotal to an understanding of the canyon itself.

The San Juan Basin may indeed be bleak and largely devoid of human occupation, but the shallow soils and sparse vegetation overlie extensive deposits of coal and uranium. In the 1970s, many archaeologists were deployed throughout the basin to conduct surveys and record sites that would be threatened by mining and road-building activities. They began locating and recording Chacoan great houses far outside the canyon itself. Called Chacoan outliers, these sites are heterogeneous with respect to their size and some architectural features. Most are more than one story, but some are not. Some outliers are isolated structures, while others stand in the midst of small villages. Nevertheless, the outliers do share certain character-

Archaeologists believe the carefully engineered Chacoan road system dates from the 11th and 12th centuries. The roads connect outlying communities to Chaco Canyon. Lacking wheeled vehicles, the Chacoan road builders had no need to construct roads with gradual turns and curves. When roads change direction, they do so with sharp, angled turns. This aerial view shows remnants of Anasazi roads, cut by deeper modern roadways, converging on the ruins of Pueblo Alto.

The Anasazi refused to allow the presence of natural obstructions such as cliffs to hinder them. They extended their roads by carving staircases—ranging from rudimentary toe- and fingerholds to full-scale flights of steps—into the sheer rock walls of the cliffs.

istics. They are built with Chacoan-style masonry, have ceramic assemblages like those at the great houses in the canyon, and have a great kiva, a tower kiva, or both. Finally, although they are all located beyond Chaco Canyon itself, they are linked to Chaco Canyon by means of a prehistoric roadway or a visual communication system.

The Navajo residents and the early archaeologists who worked there have known for decades that prehistoric roadways occurred in Chaco Canyon. Harold S. Gladwin, a major figure among the archaeologists, reported that Navajo living in Chaco Canyon thought the Anasazi had used the roads to move timbers into the canyon. Neil Judd referred to the same roads as ceremonial highways. The 1970s brought the revelation that the roadways extended far beyond the canyon confines. As part of a 15-year, multidisciplinary National Park Service project in Chaco Canyon, archaeologists began mapping the roads from aerial photographs. Later, projects largely sponsored by the Bureau of Land Management conducted additional ground surveys and some archaeological testing. Various estimates of the extent of the roads have been published. At one extreme is the figure of 1500 miles (2400 kilometers) of ancient roadways. This large number includes all segments mapped from photographs whether or not they have been checked on the ground. The most conservative estimate, based solely on segments known through "ground truth," is far less, but still more than 130 miles (208 kilometers) in length.

The most consistent feature of the prehistoric roads is their straight course. The roads are not contoured to topographic relief. Changes in direction are accomplished by a sharp angular turn rather than a curve. When the roads approach a major topographic obstacle, such as a cliff or ledge, they become stairways or ramps. The stairways vary in form from shallow, pecked finger- and toe-holds, to masonry steps consisting of two or three stones piled in front of a rock ledge, to well-constructed flights of wide steps with treads and risers cut out of the bedrock. Ramps are either stone or earth-filled masonry structures that may occur in conjunction with stairways or with road segments interrupted by ledges.

The roads vary in form and degree of preparation. Some were cut into bedrock or through wind-blown soil, but most were simply created by removing vegetation, loose soil, and debris. Some road segments are lined with masonry borders, while others are visible only as slight swales on the landscape. The widths of the roads are also distinctive and variable. Major roads are up to about 30 feet (9 meters) in width, secondary roads about 13 feet (4 meters) wide. The degree of formality and the width of the roads are greatest in the immediate vicinity of Chaco Canyon itself or the distant outlier.

Some roads appear to lead to specific areas where the resources that were brought into Chaco Canyon—salt, timber, stone, pottery—were acquired. In other instances, particularly outside the San Juan Basin, there is less evidence that these roadways, physically associated with Chacoan outliers, are connected to other roads or lead to Chaco Canyon. In these situations, it has been suggested that the road segments may represent an ideological affiliation with the canyon rather than an economic or political connection to the larger system.

In addition to the surveys of the 1970s, two large, multiyear excavation projects contributed greatly to the current understanding of Chaco as a node in a much larger regional network. The Park Service's Chaco Project, first under the direction of Robert H. Lister and, following his retirement, led by W. James Judge, excavated Pueblo Alto—a 312-room great house on the mesa top above Pueblo Bonito and Chetro Ketl. Pueblo Alto was selected for excavation, in part, because several prehistoric roads lead into it from the north and because road segments link it to both Pueblo Bonito and Chetro Ketl. It was a logical choice in order to understand prehistoric trade, exchange, and interaction.

The second major excavation was Cynthia Irwin-Williams's study of Salmon Ruin, one of only two great houses outside the canyon that are as large as Pueblo Bonito and Chetro Ketl. The other enormous outlier, Aztec Ruin, had been excavated by Earl Morris between 1916 and 1926. Data obtained through both the Salmon and Alto projects indicated considerable trade and interaction within the San Juan Basin. For example, high-quality chert, which came from distinctive sources such as New Mexico's Brushy Basin or Narbona Pass and was used for flaked stone tools, occurred in higher frequencies in the great houses than would normally be expected, either

Pueblo Bonito was built in stages, and in its final stage stood at least four stories high and contained about 600 rooms and 40 kivas. One of the largest Anasazi sites, it was in use from the early 900s to about A.D. 1200.

because of their distance from the source areas or their size. Similarly, some ceramics were tempered with sanidine basalt, a material that does not occur naturally at Chaco Canyon or in the central basin. The sanidine basalt pottery also was found to be more abundant at the great houses. Thousands of sanidine-basalt tempered pottery vessels were brought into the canyon. The basalt probably comes from sources in the Chuska Mountains of New Mexico. Considering that the central basin itself was by this time virtually devoid of wood, it is possible that pots were made at high-elevation locations, such as the Chuskas, because these had the wood resources needed to fire the pottery. As noted above, the wood used in construction also suggested exchange or interaction on a significant scale.

Until these discoveries, it had been assumed that, like modern Pueblo villages, all prehistoric pueblos had been economically and politically autonomous units. Similarities between pueblos were attributed either to shared cultural behavior, rather vague notions of "influence" from one area to another, or to migrations. During the 1970s those perceptions changed, and communities were considered as participants in a much larger, regionally based organization. Judge defined the Chacoan regional system as "a number of interacting but geographically separate communities that were dependent on each other through the exchange of goods and services." He considered the great houses in Chaco Canyon to have been central to this system during the Bonito phase of the 11th century.

Clan kivas at Pueblo Bonito are mostly about 25 feet (7.5 meters) in diameter. In their day, each kiva would have been roofed with pine timbers. These had to be imported from considerable distances. Kivas may have been used for meetings and ceremonies, and were accessible by means of a ladder, the end of which protruded from an opening in the roof. Pueblo Bonito also has two great kivas, capable of holding hundreds of people at a time.

A variety of scenarios have been developed to describe the events that took place in Chaco Canyon and the San Juan Basin between about A.D. 850-900 and 1175. There are also several explanations that attempt to explain why these events happened. All of these models depend upon paleoclimatic reconstructions, general anthropological knowledge about how societies are organized, and some basic judgments about how productive or how marginal Chaco Canyon was in terms of agriculture. An important shared element of all these models is that they consider movement to another area to be the most effective solution to declining agricultural yields or shortfalls, but that this option was precluded by regional population densities that were in place by A.D. 700. In other words, by that date the lands available were already occupied by so many Anasazi that group mobility or relocation was impossible. New solutions were required.

Chacoans built terraces, like the example shown here, along the north side of the canyon to trap seasonal runoff from rainfall and melting snow as it tumbled off the mesa top. The water was used by Anasazi farmers to irrigate gardens, and any surplus drained off into Chaco Wash. This water-control system also kept precious soil from being washed away.

Vivian and other investigators, such as Judge, have pointed out that within the marginally productive San Juan Basin as a whole, Chaco Canyon is a potential oasis because runoff water is derived from surrounding higher land masses. Rains falling at virtually any of the areas of higher elevation around the basin potentially will provide water for Chaco Canyon. As part of the Chaco Project, the Tree-Ring Laboratory at the University of Arizona developed a model of past precipitation for Chaco, permitting the reconstruction of rainfall patterns back to about A.D. 850. According to these data, the Classic Bonito period of A.D. 1000 to 1130 was relatively wet, a time when farmers in Chaco would have been unusually successful.

The unique architecture of the prehistoric Chacoan great houses and the outliers did not develop simultaneously. Archaeologists Thomas C. Windes and Dabney Ford, who have taken samples of wood from Chacoan buildings and studied tree-ring dates from Chacoan construction, note that some great-house sites in the canyon and among the outliers have older—or core—sections that date to the late 800s and reveal interesting patterning. The site plans for these early structures are remarkably like the very large Pueblo I sites: Site 13 on Alkali Ridge, for instance, and Grass Mesa Village and McPhee Pueblo of the Dolores area of southern Colorado. These early portions of great houses have suites of big rooms that are not thought to have been habitations because they lack features such as ash pits and hearths commonly found in rooms where people lived. The floor areas for rooms in these suites, ranging between 270 and 580 square feet (25 and 54 square

meters), are two-thirds larger than those of typical Chacoan small houses of the same period. The lack of habitation features argues against the sites' having been simply scaled-up versions of domestic sites. Windes and Ford suggest that they were used for storage.

The three earliest great houses in Chaco Canyon—Pueblo Bonito, Una Vida, and Peñasco Blanco—were at first shaped like other very large Pueblo I sites, such as those at Alkali Ridge. Each of these sites is located at the confluence of major drainages with Chaco Wash. As such, W. James Judge suggests they may have controlled the agricultural land associated with these drainages and therefore may have accumulated a significant surplus, thanks to the relatively benign rainfall regime of the time. Ceramics discovered in the canyon dating from this period are related to those of the southern part of the basin. Judge suggests that in addition to surplus agricultural production, the sites in Chaco Canyon began to play a central role in the processing of turquoise. Turquoise does not occur naturally within Chaco Canyon, or in the San Juan Basin. The closest source area is found in the Cerrillos Hills in the Galisteo Basin south of Santa Fe. Nevertheless, turquoise was processed at 10th-century sites in Chaco Canyon, and Judge suggests that in obtaining turquoise and turning it into finished items important in ritual, the residents of Chaco may have been developing a commodity that could be exchanged for food when conditions worsened.

During the 11th and the beginning of the 12th centuries, the climatic data indicate variable conditions for agriculture, followed by a period during which rainfall was relatively abundant for sustained intervals. This was also a time when new construction burgeoned in Chaco Canyon and when the older sites were enlarged. Judge notes that a direct connection with the confluence of drainages no longer exists among the new great houses, such as Pueblo Alto. Other considerations seem more important to site locations, and Judge maintains that these were related to ritual. In his view, due to economic conditions in the basin at the time, Chaco's emergence as a major center was tied to the nonmaterial aspects of society. He sees Chaco as serving a primary ritual function, with turquoise as the durable item of symbolic value. Judge states that in the A.D. 1000s, periodic visits to the canyon by Anasazi from throughout the region to obtain turquoise became increasingly formal as a kind of ritual metaphor. Concurrently, alliances with the outlying communities would become a more acknowledged way of integrating communities through exchange of nonritual material goods. Finally, according to Judge, "as the system became formalized—that is, as it began to develop into a true system—administration of the exchange networks would have become necessary and could easily have fallen to those residents of Chaco Canyon, particularly if turquoise was the primary material symbol of the ritual and was controlled by the residents of Chaco."

During the period of favorable moisture conditions, between 1045 and 1080, construction at the canyon's great houses increased tremendously, but most of the building consisted of storage rooms. Judge notes that the population of the canyon at this time was not very great. Observing that there were facilities in the canyon for many more people than probably lived there permanently, he argues that the canyon had become a locus for periodic pilgrimages, during which special centers distributed food and other goods during religious functions.

The McElmo phase in the canyon, and in the basin, began with a series of changes that indicate a reorganization of the Chacoan system. New structures were built in "McElmo" style. These buildings are compact, generally lacking open plaza areas and more closely resembling structures in the northern San Juan area. Rooms and passageways in older buildings at Chaco were subdivided into smaller spaces. There was a renewed intensity of village site construction. Judge suggests that these changes, in addition to the abundance of Chaco-McElmo Black-on-white pottery, indicate that Chaco was no longer central to the organization of the region. Rather, Chaco seems to have become, once again—and after a long period of time—primarily residential. The focus of a different kind of regional organization that emerged at this time, Judge proposes, may have been at Aztec or Salmon, one of the two huge northern outliers. Judge emphasizes the observation that activity in Chaco Canyon did not decline at this time. In fact, it may have increased with a larger, fully resident population. However, Chaco was no longer the ideological or principal center of the region.

Finally, a major drought that began in 1130 and lasted for 50 years coincided with decline and change in the Chacoan regional system. The evidence for these changes is a lack of new construction in the canyon and at some outliers after 1130. There is also a hiatus in trash removal at some sites, such as Pueblo Alto. Judge notes that the "end" of the Chacoan system does not appear to coincide with evidence of violence in the canyon itself. The abandonment of structures seems to have been orderly, and those who left took most of their useful items with them. Judge suggests that the end of the system was triggered by environmental factors, perhaps further encouraged by prior "supersaturation" of the canyon. In this, his discussion is similar to that proposed by LeBlanc for the Mimbres collapse. Judge maintains that the success of the Chacoan system may have brought many more people into the canyon than it could support, even periodically, if resources diminished. The Chaco decline is, in part, attributable to its success.

In overview, Judge's model for Chaco emphasizes the basin's variable climatic conditions and the ability of some of its residents to buffer the effects of that variability by virtue of their location at the confluence of two drainage systems. Later on, they made up for crop deficits by producing turquoise objects neeed for ritual. The florescence of Chaco is attributed to its role in bringing food into the canyon and redistributing it through periodic pilgrimage fairs. Judge's scenario, like some others, characterizes the entire basin and Chaco itself as marginal for agriculture. Hedging against local shortages in

After A.D. 1130, the Chaco Canyon building and pottery styles began to resemble those of Mesa Verde. Instead of thin veneer, masons used blocky sandstone elements, as shown at right. On pottery, wide dark lines replaced the thin hatching of the Classic Chacoan period, as clearly shown on the ladle below.

production is accomplished largely through the mechanism of redistributing food. Redistribution is a general form of exchange, described in the larger, general ethnographic literature. It requires that food be amassed in one place and then given out according to the social rules of the particular society. The exchange, which can be complicated, is facilitated by having it occur in the course of fulfilling social and ritual obligations.

A different view is offered by archaeologist Lynne Sebastian, who used the rainfall information provided by the Tree-Ring Laboratory to develop a computer simulation of annual crop yields. Her study shows that severe crop deficits were infrequent during the Early Bonito phase. She proposes that the agricultural surpluses accumulated during the Early Bonito phase were used opportunistically by local leaders of the early great-house communities in order to establish dependency relationships among less fortunate villages. By virtue of their abundant crops, the Chacoan leaders could "afford" to provide feasts and festivals for their poorer neighbors, in return for the loyalty these neighbors then would owe them. Furthermore, the leaders used their generosity to compete for followers.

During the 11th century, Sebastian argues, power in Chaco was related to religious knowledge, but particular leaders attracted followers by their success in competitive displays of power and wealth. The results are primarily visible today in architecture. She maintains that the great houses eventually resembled hulks of featureless rooms, many built and sited so as to emphasize their mass rather than to serve specific functions. In the same way, she states, the roads, the elaborate veneer walls, the wooden floors, wooden roofs and "wainscoting in a treeless desert, all appear to be construction for the sake of ostentation."

Sebastian argues that the outlying communities may reflect one of two possible situations. Some may have been the client communities of particular Chacoan leaders, owing periodic labor and continuing loyalty. Others, she suggests, may have organized themselves in order to mimic the successful postures of the Chacoan leaders, a behavior documented in anthropological literature elsewhere.

In contrast to Judge, Sebastian considers Chaco Canyon itself as something of an oasis in a poor and unpredictable area. She believes that leaders use whatever they can to consolidate and further expand their power, and she suggests that if they are successful, others outside the system may use the trappings of that success to their own advantage. A still different perspective is offered by Gwinn Vivian.

Vivian considers that the differences between the great-house communities and the villages in Chaco were, at least initially, a result of two different ethnic populations from separate geographic derivations. One group would have originated south of Chaco in the Red Mesa area, the other north of Chaco in the San Juan River country. Vivian's blueprint for the development of Chaco and its place in the region depends upon an analogy he makes between the presence of irrigation features in association with the great houses of Chaco and the kind of organization present among the Rio Grande Pueblos, where irrigation agriculture had long been practiced. Vivian argues that an attempt to explain the presence of prehistoric roadways in Chaco Canyon in economic terms is largely untenable, because there are several instances in which roads run parallel to one another for miles for no apparent reason. Unlike some who see the great houses as largely empty ceremonial constructs, Vivian regards both great houses and villages as primarily residential. The great-house populations are differentiated because they managed, as well as profited from, the runoff irrigation systems, which he discovered.

Vivian's explanation for the regional aspects of the Chacoan system—roads and outlier communities—is that they were established by groups from Chaco Canyon looking for better farmland on the more productive edges of the San Juan Basin. The outliers often were established within existing small-house communities, but were linked to the canyon by roads serving functional and symbolic purposes. Their symbolic function was to connect certain outliers with their parent villages or, more generally, their Chacoan homeland.

In all of these scenarios, the failure of Chaco and the regional system is linked to the major drought that began in 1130. If, prior to this time, almost any agricultural strategy was seen to work, by 1140 or 1150 the drought was so severe that virtually nothing worked. However the system functioned, it did manage to produce agricultural surpluses in some years, and these stores fed the workers, at least while they built and plastered walls, carried timbers, and ground turquoise beads. Surplus agricultural production was not possible anywhere during the 1130s and 1140s—or, if some small surplus could be produced, perhaps no one wanted to use it to pay for the trappings of the failed management.

Some of the Pueblo peoples have oral histories about the ruins their ancestors left behind, although none of the modern villages claims the sites in Chaco Canyon specifically. In the Hopi histories, nearly invariably, the world is destroyed or villages are abandoned when people who had plenty to eat began to gamble and neglected their obligations to one another and to their gods. Things became too easy and people became frivolous. Abandonment follows abundance in these stories.

The Navajo have a legend about the Anasazi of Chaco Canyon. It tells us that the people of Chaco were too rigid and uncompromising. They had too many rules. The failure is thus a social failure, one in which the social institutions are not appropriate.

None of the different scenarios offers a very satisfactory explanation. They do not rely on physical laws or on cultural patterns that are familiar enough to allow prediction or richer understanding of other aspects of the Chacoan archaeological record. Yet the stories may lead us to think of ways these aspects might be evaluated. Alternatively, the stories of what might have happened may help us think about Chaco Canyon and the San Juan Basin in human terms, terms that are more accessible to us than empty great kivas and silent sandstone walls. Chaco is there for us to people in our imaginations. It is at the end of the road and in the middle of nowhere in a symbolic as well as a physical sense. Its presence suggests that we must build a path to Chaco beyond the current state of our scientific knowledge. We may spend time in Chaco today to seek inspiration for that path, and undoubtedly we will require time in Chaco to test and evaluate the ideas we develop about the ways it came into being, worked, and failed.

Framed by sandstone, the remains of Cliff Palace—the largest cliff dwelling in Mesa Verde National Park—show some of this site's 220 rooms are large and well-constructed, Mesa Verde sites reflect an aggregation of dwellings rather than the planned sites typical of Chaco Canyon.

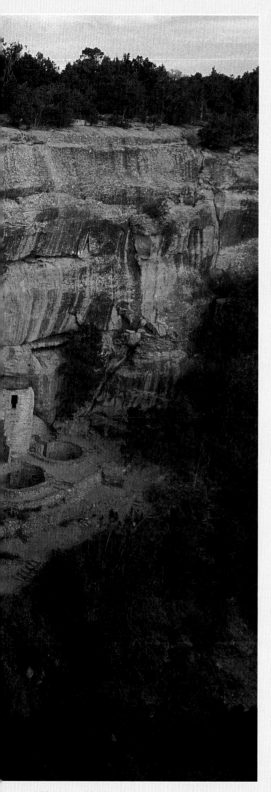

and 23 kivas. Although the sandstone structures

7

GREAT PUEBLO: A TIME OF TRANSITION

The period from A.D. 1150 to 1300 was one of enormous change in both the Mogollon and Anasazi regions. In the Pecos Classification, it is referred to as Great Pueblo, an appropriate reference to the size of the pueblos built during this period. The large village ruins of this interval are the emblems and icons of the guidebooks on Pueblo prehistory, symbolizing ancient Pueblo culture for most of the world. According to Alfred Kidder, this was not a time of major technological innovations, but

Great Pueblo (circa A.D. 1150 to 1300) was a time of consolidation and refinement. The territory occupied by the Anasazi shrank, but the period also saw the construction of some of the most famous Pueblos. By the end of Great Pueblo, the Anasazi had abandoned the Four Corners region.

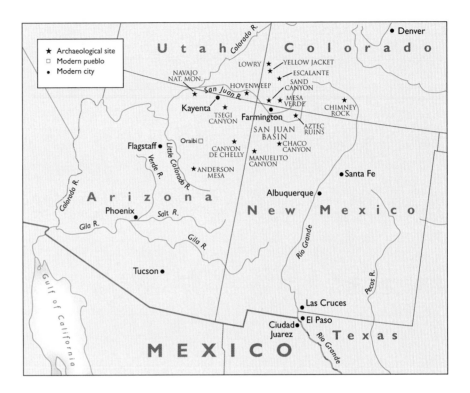

rather a time when Pueblo building skills, crafts, and domestic arts were refined. Great Pueblo sites include Cliff Palace, Spruce Tree House, and other prominent ruins of Mesa Verde, the oldest archaeological National Park in the United States; White House and Antelope House of Canyon de Chelly; and Betatakin and Kiet Siel of Navajo National Monument. Many of the ruins are cliff dwellings, sheltered from the elements and preserved beneath rock overhangs, allowing the preservation of the small and vivid details that bring their builders to life in our imaginations.

As we have already seen, the coming together of once-dispersed people into large settlements may, on a different scale, be viewed as instances of abandonment. Smaller settlements are deserted when larger ones are formed. The founding of many Great Pueblo communities came about as scores of smaller, Pueblo II settlements were abandoned. The enormous territory over which Pueblo II sites had been established drastically shrinks in the Great Pueblo period. The withdrawal of Pueblo agriculturists from the edges of the ancient Pueblo world generally is attributed to a complex set of environmental events that took place between 1130 and 1180. The same environmental factors also destabilized the integration of the Chacoan regional system, and the failure of the Chacoan organization, in turn, created a wave of abandonments among the smaller communities scattered throughout the San Juan Basin.

The end of the Great Pueblo period in A.D. 1300 is marked by the final, complete abandonment of most of the traditional Anasazi and Mogollon territories: the entire Four Corners region, the Mimbres Valley, Forestdale, and Pine Lawn areas. This continues to be one of the greatest mysteries in our knowledge of the prehistoric Southwest, but one aspect of the abandonment is not an enigma. There is no question that the descendants of those who abandoned the former Great Pueblo settlements live today among the modern Pueblo villages of Arizona and New Mexico.

Multidisciplinary research efforts carried out in the 1980s have greatly enhanced our understanding of environmental conditions across the Colorado Plateaus during the Great Pueblo period. Tree rings record a region-wide drought that began in A.D. 1130. This dry interval persisted until about 1180. In addition to the drought, the period from about 1100 to 1200 was a time when water tables throughout the plateaus were dropping. The environmental processes that underlie the decline in water tables are not related to those that affect precipitation, so that there is not necessarily a correlation between the two conditions. The fact that the drought coincided with lowered water tables was an unlucky coincidence for ancient Pueblo farmers.

There are also differences in the timing of drought and water-table changes that have implications for human behavior. Major rises and falls in water tables cycle slowly—much more slowly than the cycles of rainfall variation. Differences in rainfall patterning occur from year to year and are easily recognized. Farmers can offset the potential loss of crops by increasing the amount of food that is stored during good years and by overplanting. Changes in water-table levels, on the other hand, affect whether or not streams are eroding headward and cutting deeper channels. There are cycles in these hydrologic curves, but they last longer than a human generation, so changes in water tables are not easily perceived. Consequently, people cannot plan effective strategies to compensate for the erosion that results from declining water tables.

The co-occurrence of drought and a cycle of erosion in the middle 1100s must have been devastating. Erosion, headward cutting of arroyos, and down cutting of streams decrease the amount of land that can be used for cultivation. If one strategy for coping with drought was to plant in and near arroyo beds, or in a variety of different kinds of settings, with the hope that some fields at least would be successful, then the loss of land to erosion would have greatly diminished the strategy's potential for success. There are well-documented historic cases in which arroyo cutting has drastically and irreversibly reduced the area of farmland, with consequent and severe effects on the farmers involved. In one well-known example, 800 acres (325 hectares) of the best farmland available to the Hopi village of Oraibi were lost between 1907 and 1912.

Whether or not the combination of drought, lowered water tables, and erosion was perceived by the Pueblo ancestors as elements in the abandon-

ments of the late 1100s, many localities on the edges of the Pueblo homeland were deserted. The territory at the farthest western extent of Pueblo
land, including southwestern Utah, the southern tip of Nevada, and the
Arizona strip, seems to have been deserted very gradually, over a period of
more than 100 years. Archaeologists have attributed this abandonment to
climatic deterioration.

Abandonment also took place in major portions of western and northwestern Mogollon territory. In some cases, this occurred as a local consequence of
aggregation. For example, in the Grasshopper region, villages were burned, an
indication that a coming together appears to have taken place as a consequence
of warfare. Both the congregating and the conflict may have been indirect
responses to drought and declining agricultural yields.

Betatakin occupies a spectacular cave location in Tsegi Canyon. This site was settled, expanded, and abandoned in less than two generations. To compensate for the sloping cave floor, the builders carved out spaces for wall foundations and piled dirt and trash behind retaining walls.

Life in Chaco Canyon changed dramatically after 1150. Thenceforward, no Chacoan great houses were built, and the evidence of occupation in the canyon is so different that it is difficult to recognize. Archaeologist Peter McKenna, summarizing the post-1150 occupation in Chaco, notes that it is largely represented by artifacts scattered on structures that had been built considerably earlier. What new construction did take place in the canyon consisted of small storage structures in the cliffs and, probably, the addition of great kivas to Pueblo Bonito, Chetro Ketl, and the village community at Casa Rinconada. A single 40-room pueblo on top of Fajada Butte, an imposing land form in the central canyon, also may have been built after 1150. It is interesting to speculate that the investment in additional storage space and facilities for ritual activity were both aimed at ameliorating the impacts of drought and erosion.

Given the Southwest's general aridity and climatic variability, there is a strong inclination among archaeologists to credit environmental factors as primary causes of cultural change. But it is likely that the causal roles of other factors have been underestimated. A better understanding of some cultural factors that have been slighted in archaeological writing comes through an examination of the process of aggregation on a regional scale. As the geographic peripheries of the old Pueblo world were gradually abandoned, other long-inhabited areas witnessed major population increases and the establishment of their largest settlements.

Archaeologist Jeffrey Dean has conducted intensive studies in dendrochronology and paleoclimatic reconstruction, as well as surveys and excavations, in the Kayenta area. He observed that in A.D. 1150 many areas were abandoned, but in those locations that continued to be inhabited, high population densities and large settlements developed. Very few sites dating between A.D. 1150 and 1250 have been excavated in the Kayenta area. It was during this interval, however, that soil and water conservation features (such as grid borders, terraces, check dams, etc.) were first built here. Settlements of two different forms occur. One consists of a few scattered pithouses associated with a masonry-lined kiva. The other settlement type is the more traditional pueblo of stone masonry room blocks facing a plaza. In some locations, such as Navajo Mountain, the pueblo type is the most common form. Both types are found in the Tsegi Canyon-Marsh Pass area.

In the Kayenta area, the period between A.D. 1250 and 1300 is called the Tsegi phase, and more is known of this time than any other in the region. Tsegi is an anglicized pronunciation of the Navajo *Tséyi'*. The Spanish pronunciation of the same word is Chelly, giving us the geographical terms Tsegi Canyon and Canyon de Chelly. Not surprisingly, one translation of Navajo Tséyi' is "among the rocks," or "water flows out among rocks," which is a common way of referring to a canyon. Most Tsegi phase sites are open, constructed in a variety of settings on mesa tops and valley floors. Valley floor settlements cluster tightly on the landscape. Within the well-known National Monuments of Canyon de Chelly and Navajo National Monument, however, the Tsegi phase sites were built in cliffs under rock overhangs. Two of the most spectacular Tsegi phase sites are Betatakin (Ledge House in Navajo) and Kiet Siel (Broken Pottery in Navajo), both in the Tsegi Canyon system of Navajo National Monument. Although the two sites are only a few miles apart, were occupied at the same time, and share virtually all aspects of material culture, they have different histories of occupation. These were worked out by Jeffrey Dean.

Betatakin occupies a spectacular setting in an alcove 450 feet (137 meters) high and 370 feet (112 meters) across, above a dense stand of aspen and oak thicket. The initial settlement of Betatakin seems to have been planned. The first three or four households to settle arrived between A.D. 1267 and 1268, cutting and stockpiling timbers to use as beams. In 1277, these beams were used to

Kiet Siel, shown at right and above, is the largest cliff dwelling in Arizona and also the best preserved. Here, several household groups occupied clusters of rooms. Sandstone masonry walls were used for most construction, but within a single household, rooms or work spaces might be divided with walls of *jacal*—poles set vertically and covered with mud. In the photo above, only the poles remain. Kiet Siel was founded in 1250, and the period of greatest growth occurred between 1272 and 1276. By 1300 the dwelling was completely abandoned.

Parts of Antelope House in Canyon de Chelly, seen at right, were built in 1075. The name of the site refers to the four life-size paintings of antelope, created by Navajo artists during the 1800s, on the cliff face above and west of the ruin. Two of these, along with quadrupeds, concentric circles, and other rock art made by the Anasazi during the 1200s, are visible in the photo below.

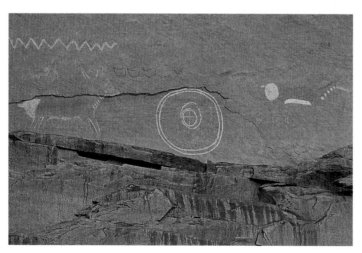

build rooms by a group of perhaps 75 to 100 people. Following this influx, Betatakin grew more slowly, reaching a peak of about 125 inhabitants. Only one rectangular kiva was found at Betatakin, although there is also a smaller rectangular kiva in an alcove farther up the canyon that may have been used by the Betatakin residents. The last beam was cut at Betatakin in 1286, and shortly thereafter the residents left their spectacular cliff shelter. In less than two generations the entire site had been founded, had flourished, and been abandoned.

Kiet Siel, the largest cliff dwelling in Arizona, is so well preserved that most of the roofs and some jacal walls are intact. The ruin gives a visitor the feeling that its occupants have left only weeks before. In fact, Kiet Siel was founded in 1250. The village grew slowly for the first 12 years. Then there was an influx of people between 1272 and 1276. Thereafter, the site grew in fits and starts. Rooms were added, modified, and abandoned as needed until 1286, when construction ceased. Like Betatakin, Kiet Siel was deserted by 1300.

This remarkably preserved cradleboard, found at Antelope House in Canyon de Chelly, is 700 years old. The woven cotton cradle band passed over the baby's stomach, holding the child securely in place. At the start of the Pueblo period, the Anasazi began strapping their babies to hard wooden cradleboards, a practice that produced artificially flattened skulls—presumably an aesthetically desirable trait. Cradleboards were used throughout the Pueblo period, and are still used by some traditional Navajo people today.

Although it is organized along formal "streets," Kiet Siel shows more architectural diversity than does Betatakin. Masonry and jacal walls were built, and the four round kivas differ one from another in certain details. Two granaries were painted with broad bands of white paint that match those in a keyhole-shaped kiva. Possibly, the granaries contained corn for use on ceremonial occasions, or perhaps to support a particular group of people who shared responsibility for the kiva's rituals. A D-shaped room with its straight wall of jacal is also associated with this kiva. It is one of two such rooms, considered "ceremonial annexes," where particular, perhaps more public, rituals took place. Mesa Verde connections are suggested by rooms built late in the occupation of Kiet Siel. One of the rooms is a two-story tower kiva of Mesa Verde type. The other is the keyhole-shaped kiva, a prevalent shape at Mesa Verde.

The contrast in numbers of kivas—six at Kiet Siel, one at Betatakin—and their differences in shape—round at Kiet Siel, rectangular at Betatakin—are striking. Perhaps the residents of Betatakin continued to use their ancestral village for some ceremonial activities, and that village may have been close by. The residents of Kiet Siel may have had closer ties to people in Mesa Verde, a place too distant to visit on a regular basis.

In Canyon de Chelly National Monument, a portion of Antelope House Ruin was built in A.D. 1075, before the drought of 1130 and the Tsegi phase. The site was very carefully and systematically excavated in the early 1970s. Antelope House Ruin was named for the spectacular, life-size pictographic rendering of four antelope on the cliff face west of the ruin. These magnificent paintings were made by the Navajo in the early 1800s, long after the site itself had become a mound of rubble.

If Antelope House had been named for its most salient Kayenta Anasazi characteristic, it might have been called Cotton House. The 1970s excavations at Antelope House yielded more than 1100 specimens of cotton textiles, totaling about 15.5 square yards (12.8 square meters) of cloth. In addition, some 4.4 pounds (1.9 kilograms) of raw cotton, including bolls, seeds, fiber, and twigs, were recovered in a sample of excavated material. This abundance suggests that Antelope House may have been a local or regional center for weaving, thus providing unique evidence of craft specialization among the Post-Chaco Anasazi. The recovery of the cotton is also a tribute to careful excavation and the excellent preservation conditions under the overhanging cliffs. Among the textiles recovered are woven belts, aprons, blankets, tumplines, breechcloth fronts, and cradle bands. One remarkable find from Antelope House is a cradleboard with a woven cradle band that was used to hold the infant gently and securely in place.

Construction at Antelope House Ruin began at the south end of the site. Subsequently, room blocks were added in the central and northern sections of the site. Eventually, Antelope House grew to contain about 80 rooms and five kivas. The older, southern room block area was the only part of the site in which multistory construction was common, with 12 upper-story units of four stories each.

National Park Service archaeologist Don P. Morris interprets the sequence of construction and the choices made by the builders as evidence that two different social groups occupied Antelope House, with the Central Plaza serving an integrating function after about A.D. 1200. By noting a number of differences in room sizes, the use of plaster, and kiva wall art, as well as minor variations in pottery designs and basketry weaving, Morris inferred that the Central Plaza at Antelope House may have brought together two social groups inhabiting the site or may have linked comparable groups outside the archaeologically recognized boundaries of the site.

A universal human symbol, handprint motifs made with clay and mineral colors are common throughout all periods, especially in the western Anasazi area (including Canyon de Chelly). Ethnographic studies support the idea that the prints were a means of personal identification.

Among the canyon's most evocative remains is the rock art, much of which dates to earlier Anasazi times. Handprint motifs made with clay and mineral colors are common throughout the Anasazi occupation. Many of the images, though, are associated with the Tsegi-phase cliff dwellings, and must have been part of the daily lives of their inhabitants. There are both petroglyphs and very large paintings done on clay. Among the latter is a circular painting on white near Betatakin that has been interpreted by the Hopi as a symbol of their Fire Clan. The negative image is seen as Masauwu, the Hopi god of earth and death who is also the controller of fire. Other characteristic figures are lizards and lizard-men, figures that the Zuni believe represent Pueblo people shortly after their emergence from the underworld and before they became fully human.

Around 1300, when the people left Tsegi Canyon and Canyon de Chelly, many probably traveled south and west to new, very large villages being founded on Anderson Mesa and in the Middle Little Colorado River area. These late prehistoric villages are known by, and considered ancestral communities of, the Hopi especially and also the Zuni people.

Outside Chaco Canyon, but still within the San Juan Basin, in the country that had been dominated by Chacoan outliers, there were great episodes of building after 1150. Over the last eight years a major archaeological effort to survey and prepare detailed maps of sites in this vast territory was completed by archaeologists John Stein and Andrew Fowler. They, along with Roger Anyon, director of the archaeology program at Zuni Pueblo, have developed a

Twin Towers Ruin in Hovenweep National Monument, Utah, is typical of the many towers built by Pueblo III people in the Larger Mesa Verde region. Although some towers may well have served defensive purposes, others are located in swales or in cliffs, with no view of the surrounding terrain. The towers are connected to kivas, sometimes by means of a tunnel, suggesting that their primary functions may have been ceremonial and religious.

chronology useful for describing the post-1150 events of the region. As Stein and Anyon note, the immediate Post-Chaco Era was one of the poorest known in the entire Anasazi chronology. They define the Post-Chaco Era as the period between A.D. 1150 and 1250. During this time, core-veneer masonry continues to be used, but there are no kiva depressions incorporated into room blocks. A great kiva is located outside the room block area and a compound wall may enclose a large plaza. Some great houses of the Post-Chaco Era are associated with roadways.

Stein, Fowler, and Anyon recognize a Big House period from A.D. 1250 to 1300. Big Houses retain core-veneer masonry and, in contrast to the preceding period, kivas are again located in room block areas. Unlike earlier great houses, the Big Houses are set off from surrounding terrain by berms or masonry barriers that have formal entries into an enclosed plaza. Stein, Fowler and Anyon acknowledge that the great houses and Big Houses of Post-Chaco times incorporated some residential space. They argue, however, that it would be an error to conclude that the architecture of these communities was not public, formal, and ceremonial. They maintain that the sustaining population incorporated by these emblematic structures was very large and dispersed. While Stein, Fowler, and Anyon do not really define the community structure of these sites, they propose that there are no analogs among the modern, politically and economically autonomous Pueblo villages.

Within the San Juan Basin, Stein and his colleagues suggest that following the completion of Aztec Pueblo in 1120, the northern edge of the old Chacoan basin became a major regional center with abundant construction of both public and residential architecture. The public architecture consists of seven nearly Chaco-style great houses and 16 great kivas. Although the great houses continue the core-veneer masonry pattern, they lack associated earth mounds or berms. The residential architecture consists of many small hamlets. Ceramics found on residential and great house sites generally post-date 1150, and are carbon painted types much like those then being made at Mesa Verde.

South of Chaco is the Mañuelito Canyon area, a marvelously rugged and remote territory, which, following a burst of archaeological investigation in the 1930s, was generally forgotten by a later generation of investigators. It was named for the Navajo leader who led his people into the canyon during the Indian Wars of the 1860s to escape capture by Col. Kit Carson and the U.S. Cavalry. There they hid, avoiding the terrible Long Walk to the Bosque Redondo, during which hundreds of Navajo and Apache perished.

Fowler and Stein have worked out the Post-Chaco sequence for Mañuelito Canyon. The period from 1150 to 1250 is represented by a site called Ats'éé Nitsaa, a name that means big navel in Navajo and refers to its great kiva. Ats'éé Nitsaa consists of a massive great house with core-veneer masonry, 10 other masonry structures, and a great kiva enclosed by a stone compound wall. The Big House period from 1250 to 1350 is represented by aptly named Big House. This structure measures 328 by 360 feet (100 by 110 meters) built on a natural hillside, creating more than 65 feet (20 meters) of vertical relief. In addition to Chacoan-style features, such as core and veneer masonry, the site also incorporates new elements, including a plaza incorporated by a wall of single-story rooms. This pattern of plaza orientation or focus is one that persists into the final prehistoric and protohistoric periods of Pueblo development.

Although Mesa Verde itself is justifiably renowned worldwide for its cliff dwellings, in fact it is only one small part of a larger region of exceptionally dense occupation during the Great Pueblo period. The entire region would include the cliff dwellings and open sites of Hovenweep National Monument and Ute Mountain Tribal Park in southeastern Utah and the Ackmen-Lowry, Escalante, Chimney Rock, Sand Canyon, and Yellow Jacket area ruins of southwestern Colorado. This huge region of the northern San Juan was occupied by the Anasazi from at least A.D. 500 until 1300. Based on room counts and site counts, their numbers apparently grew over much of that time. Not until the Post-Chaco Era of A.D. 1150 to 1250 did the population of the Northern San Juan region reach its prehistoric maximum.

A number of sites in the general Mesa Verde region appear to be Big Houses of the Post-Chaco Era. Some are associated with roads, and all have substantial residential communities nearby. Examples of these would probably include Yucca House, Mud Spring Ruin, Escalante Ruin, and Lowry Ruin. It is likely

Mesa Verde kivas were typically "key-hole" shaped, with a recess behind the fireplace, and a deflector. Many Mesa Verde kivas have simple vertical walls; others, like the example from Mug House shown here, have a series of short masonry pilasters. General kiva shape or features are typical for geographic areas within the Anasazi region. However, some architectural elements, such as benches, pilasters, and niches occur more frequently in one region than another, and may be signs of social relationships that are not fully understood.

that at least some of these were established in the vicinity of existing communities. Others may not have been. An important thrust for the archaeology of the next decade or so will be understanding the relationships between Post-Chaco Era great houses and the indigenous communities surrounding them.

During the Great Pueblo period, dozens of multistory Pueblos were built. At Mesa Verde itself, these were predominantly cliff dwellings, but elsewhere they were not. The walls of Mesa Verde-style buildings are of carefully shaped, pecked, sandstone blocks, often two courses thick and laid with little mortar. Mesa Verde kivas are partially or wholly enclosed by rooms and are often key-hole-shaped. Two- to four-story towers are common at Mesa Verde, though far more so at Hovenweep. Sometimes interpreted as defensive, not all towers command a view. Some were situated at low points on the mesa tops. The towers are most often linked to a kiva, generally through a tunnel, suggesting that they may have been used for ritual.

Those dwellings constructed in rock shelters vary in form, room arrangement, and height. In part, the variation reflects the constraints of the shapes of the shallow caves. It is also true that Mesa Verde-style building was generally accretional—groups of rooms were added as needed in almost any way that would fit. At some sites, room clusters or room suite groupings can be distinguished, and seem to represent the private space of a single household. Rooms in such a cluster have doorway access to each other, but not to rooms in other clusters.

Despite the general similarity of cliff dwellings in the Mesa Verde, Tsegi Canyon, and Canyon de Chelly areas, there is a fundamental difference in the way the settlement systems must have functioned. In the western canyons, farmland is found on the canyon bottoms below the cliffs and rock shelters. At Mesa Verde, fields were on the mesa tops. Travel to and from mesa-top fields is awkward. Mesa-top fields cannot effectively be guarded from nonhuman or human predators. The use of field houses is a partial solution to these difficulties and field houses are abundant at Mesa Verde. Other agricultural features such as linear borders and check dams are also numerous. Some mesa-top sites also had water-catchment basins that may have been used as reservoirs for domestic use.

Items of material culture in the Mesa Verde area include ground and pecked stone mauls and axes, manos and metates, bone awls, chipped stone points, knives and scrapers, corrugated utility ware, and carbon black-on-white painted pottery. Great Pueblo-period Mesa Verde pottery includes abundant distinctive forms. In addition to the usual bowls and ollas (water jars), there are ladles, kiva jars, and mugs, all handsomely decorated. Pottery trade wares are generally from the Kayenta region, reinforcing the inference of close relationships between Kayenta Anasazi and Mesa Verdeans. Stone and shell pendants and beads occur, as do otherwise perishable items such as sandals, sashes, and baskets that have been preserved in cliff dwellings.

Many of the well-known Mesa Verde cliff dwellings were excavated before the use of refined field techniques became routine. Fortunately, in the 1960s, archaeologist Arthur Rohn meticulously excavated a 94-room site called Mug House, providing detail on the organizational features of the site. Mug House is situated on Wetherill Mesa, inside Mesa Verde National Park. Rohn identified four levels of organization at Mug House: room suites, courtyard units, moieties, and the community as a whole. Room suites are rooms connected by doorways, probably serving as the living and working areas of a single household. Courtyard units consist of clusters of room suites opening on a common courtyard that is also often the roof of a small kiva. Rohn reconstructed the building sequence at Mug House. Initially there was but one courtyard unit. Later, there were four units: two within Mug House Cave itself, one in nearby Adobe Cave, and a fourth at an open site in the immediate vicinity. During the latest period, these four merged into one pueblo. The existence of moieties (two groups of residences) is somewhat less convincing. During the final occupation of Mug House, there was apparently no direct access between the northern and southern halves of the pueblo. Also, the architectural features of the five kivas in the northern sector of the site are very similar, whereas the kivas in the southern part of the site do not resemble each other. The community level Rohn defines consists of the residents of Mug House and of several other contemporary settlements in the immediate vicinity who would certainly have been engaged in daily, face-to-face interaction.

Mug House, at Mesa Verde, was excavated in the late 1960s, and consists of 94 rooms. Mug House contained four levels of organization: room suites, courtyard units, moieties, and the community as a whole. The rooms clustered around a kiva, shown at right, are part of a courtyard unit. The kiva would have been roofed, providing a work area accessible from the living rooms.

In marked contrast to Mug House, at least in scale, is Sand Canyon Pueblo, a very large, aggregated, open site of at least 420 rooms, 90 kivas, 14 towers, an enclosed plaza, a D-shaped multiwalled structure, a great kiva, and various peripheral structures and features. The site was built around a spring at the head of a small canyon that bifurcates the site. Construction and occupation of Sand Canyon Pueblo took place between about 1250 and 1285. Excavations at Sand Canyon Pueblo have been directed by Bruce A. Bradley for the Crow Canyon Archeological Center, a private educational and research organization.

Bradley's studies indicate that Sand Canyon Pueblo was built to a plan initiated by the communal construction of the massive wall that encloses the site. Construction took place quickly, in the period between 1250 and the 1270s, with kiva suites consisting of a kiva, several rooms, occasionally a tower, or simply as individual kivas. In contrast, habitation rooms were added when needed. Bradley notes that Sand Canyon Pueblo consisted of both domestic and specialized, public or ritual architecture, and that the two are separated spatially. Domestic architecture is located primarily on the east side of the site. The special function, public architecture is situated predominantly on the west side of the site. Sand Canyon Pueblo is not simply an agglomeration of habitation suites, but incorporates a range of meaningful formal elements as well. How the formality relates to the local expression of Post-Chaco, Big House architecture in the Mesa Verde area remains to be more fully explored.

The remains of Long House nestle under a protective cliffside in Frijoles Canyon, New Mexico. The rows of holes visible in what were the settlement's walls once served as sockets for the roof beams, or *vigas*. Frijoles Canyon is cut into soft, easily eroded volcanic tuff, which accounts for the ruggedness of the cliff.

The latest construction dates throughout much of the Four Corners region are in the 1270s. By about 1300, the people who had built and lived in the massive stone structures were gone. Having left the cool canyon country they had occupied for 800 years, they bequeathed the mystery surrounding their departure to generations far in the future. These inheritors would generate many ingenious theories, ideas, and reasons for the exodus, but scientific substantiation of them is difficult. Drought, erosion and arroyo cutting, warfare, factionalism, and disease are the most common reasons cited for abandonment. But all have their skeptics, and none is well supported by archaeological data. Although most reasons given emphasize a single cause, it is likely that abandonments are complicated events that involve a combination of events.

One of the earliest explanations was that a major drought, documented in tree rings, had occurred between A.D. 1276 and 1299, and was the cause of the abandonments. No one disputes the existence of the drought, but its significance is not certain. Among several observations undermining the great-drought hypothesis is the fact that Tsegi Canyon sites such as Betatakin and Kiet Siel and the villages on the Hopi Mesa were all either established or continuously occupied while the drought ran its course. If the drought's consequences had been truly regional in scope, then these sites, too, should have been abandoned. Another vintage scenario combines the effects of drought with those produced by arroyo cutting as twin causal agents. Yet water-table levels were not as low in the 14th century as they had been during the 12th century. Further, hundreds of check dams and terraces in the Upper San Juan country were built prior to abandonment. They continue to retain soil and moisture today, which suggests that they were effective in curbing erosion in the past.

Warfare as another explanation for abandonment, whether against invading, hostile nomads or other Anasazi, is at least as old a conjecture as the great-drought theory. It is undeniable that some late-13th-century settlements are in highly defensive settings. Some, such as a few in Long House Valley, are virtually inaccessible. On the other hand, physical evidence of conflict, such as burned villages or skeletons bearing mortal wounds, is lacking. And who would the enemy have been? While some scholars have suggested that the ancestors of the modern Navajo and Apache attacked the Four Corners settlements, there is no evidence that these people were in the Southwest until about 1500, long after the abandonments had occurred. Others have postulated that the enemy may have been Utes, who have a longer history in the region. That idea is countered by others who claim that before Europeans introduced the horse, foraging peoples such as the Utes or the Athabascan speakers who came later would have lacked the ability to carry out swift surprise attacks and would have posed little threat to the Anasazi villagers.

Internecine warfare among the Pueblos and inter-village factionalism also have their supporters as causes of abandonment. It is true that the essential pacifism of Pueblo peoples has been much overdrawn. No large group of people is inherently peaceful. As militia, Pueblo peoples fought bravely alongside the Spaniards against nomadic tribes. Further, there is evidence of violent behavior between Pueblos. For example, from the West Pueblo at Aztec Ruin, as well as from sites on Mesa Verde and in the Animas and La Plata valleys, traumatized skeletal remains have been found in circumstances that do not conform to formal burials. However, although warfare may certainly cause the destruction of a single village—perhaps even a few villages—it does not account for abandonment of a region on the scale of the entire northern tier of Anasazi settlement.

Factionalism within Pueblo villages is known from historic and contemporary periods. One such dispute culminated in the split and near desertion of the Hopi village of Oraibi in 1906. Again, while factional disputes may have been common in the past, they do not generally lead to the abandonment of a large region. In the case of Oraibi, new villages were founded in the immediate vicinity.

A number of scholars have attributed abandonment to disease and malnutrition. It has been pointed out that population aggregation preceded abandonment in the Four Corners area and that, in densely inhabited villages, poor sanitary practices may have encouraged epidemic diseases. Unfortunately, little evidence exists either to refute or substantiate this idea. The infectious diseases that cause epidemics generally do not leave observable marks on skeletons. It has been suggested that poor nutrition and declining birthrates may have greatly reduced the Four Corners population, prompting the discouraged survivors to leave. A skeletal condition called porotic hyperostosis, which causes the bone to become pitted and spongy, occurs in Mesa Verde-area skeletons, and has been cited as evidence of malnutrition. While this may be true, modern clinical studies suggest that it is an ambiguous diagnosis. The condition also can occur as a result of short but severe childhood illnesses that do not reflect the general health of the population.

Among the most recent and controversial proposals supporting the existence of malnutrition among the Four Corners-area Anasazi has been forwarded by paleoanthropologist Tim D. White and biological anthropologist Christy G. Turner II. They have examined fragmentary human skeletal remains from sites in the Mancos Valley and from Yellow Jacket, concluding that there is evidence of cannibalism consistent with starvation. Quite reasonably, they also argue that archaeologists have not yet recognized this behavior, and it may therefore have been more widespread than is indicated in the current literature. Certainly, unless cannibalism is shown to have been far more common than the cases so far examined, it is unlikely to be linked to the major abandonments.

Over the past several years, some archaeologists have suggested that Western European ideas about settlement may color our interpretations of prehistoric abandonment. Western Europeans are accustomed to settlement stability. It is true that Rome was not built in a day, but it is also still inhabited. New York and Boston have not become ghost towns despite the growth of Los Angeles and San Diego. The landscapes of Mesopotamia, Anatolia, and the Levant are dotted with tells, or ancient mounds, which result from millennia of human occupation. In the Americas, in general, that kind of extreme settlement depth is rare. The Maya centers of Tikal, Guatemala, and Chichén Itzá in Mexico; the Mississippian sites of Cahokia near St. Louis, Missouri, and Moundville, Alabama, were all deserted before the arrival of Europeans. Because they are single sites, rather than large regions, none of these situations is comparable to the Four Corners. Yet there are parallels. Virtually all the southern lowland Maya centers were abandoned prehistorically. Perhaps our own notions of settlement permanence are somewhat skewed.

In addition to the abandonment of single settlements, a common pattern in the prehistoric Southwest was the movement of people into an adjacent area for longer or shorter periods. For example, movements up and down in elevation were apparently frequent responses to changes in rainfall patterns. Also, as indicated previously, population aggregation in a few larger settlements leaves unoccupied terrain between them of necessity. Nevertheless, the regional abandonments at the end of the 1200s did not necessarily result from an accumulation of smaller residential moves. The abandonments followed a period of population growth which accompanied the breakdown of older, regional trade ties and perhaps the replacement of formal, planned village layouts by a combination of residential and public space. In the greater Four Corners region, the abandonments did coincide with a period of less predictable and decreased precipitation.

These observations indicate that the eventual abandonment may reflect the inability of the social system to sustain dense populations. The archaeological remains can be viewed either from the perspective of continuity or of change. If continuity is emphasized, as it is by Stein, Fowler, Anyon, and others, there is a gradual transition from Chacoan great house complexes to the Post-Chaco interval with great houses and masonry-compound walls, to the Big Houses with plaza orientation and incorporation of kiva space into room-block areas. The Big Houses resemble, in these features, settlement forms of the 15th and 16th centuries. In this view, there is an Anasazi vocabulary of public architecture that shows continuity over tremendous geographic areas and long periods of time. Whether this continuity extends to key social institutions is not known.

On the other hand, if the focus is on change, geographic discontinuity is more apparent. There is the cessation of building in Chaco Canyon itself, interpreted as an instance of systemic collapse and failure. This is followed by a period of population aggregation outside the central San Juan Basin at sites interpreted as showing a general affiliation with Mesa Verde and as being predominantly residential. The abandonment of the Four Corners is then potentially linked to over-exploitation of the resource base by this greatly enlarged population. This overuse of the land, coupled either with a decrease in rainfall or climatic instability, results in the final abandonment of the region.

There is considerable merit in emphasizing continuity. It allows a basis for understanding the succeeding phases in Anasazi development. It also enables us to appreciate the factors that underlie the human decisions to leave their ancestral homelands. What can it have been like to watch kin and friends depart, knowing that there would be fewer people to help with the daily work, fewer visitors bringing news, and not enough people to hold the important ceremonies that marked the passage of lives or the change of seasons? Surely the bonds of human interaction, fellowship, and secure social life outweighed any advantages in staying.

During the late 1200s and early 1300s, a major center developed at Casas Grandes in the Mexican state of Chihuahua. With more than 200 habitation areas, and a large central courtyard that may have been a market area, this was a mercantile center, or—according to its excavator— a city,

8

A NEW PUEBLO ORDER: 1350 TO 1680

Change seems to have been the most dominant characteristic of the Pueblo world between 1350 and 1680—change in climate, change brought about by the development of new religious beliefs, changes in the social organization of communities, and the dramatic change imposed by foreign invasions.

After the major drought between 1276 and 1299, the early 1300s was a time of generally improved rainfall. Nevertheless, from 1325 to 1425 there was great variability in

rooms, effigy mounds, ball courts, workshop which he named Paquimé.

Following the abandonment of the Four Corners region after A.D. 1300, the focus of Pueblo activity shifted south, southwest, and east. This period saw the rise of Casas Grandes, a huge trading center in what is now Mexico. The advent of the Spanish in 1539 spelled irrevocable change for the Pueblos: from the late 1500s, the Rio Grande area became the focus of Spanish missionary efforts.

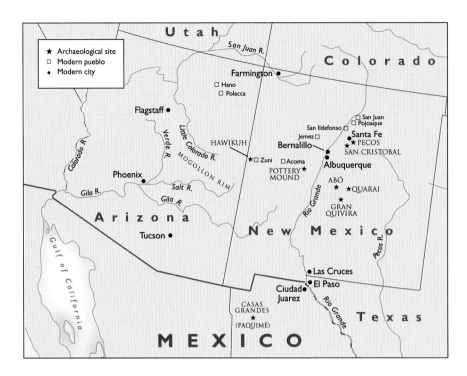

precipitation from one year to another and from one geographic area to another. In 1425, a short episode of drought began that may have undermined further expansion of Pueblo settlement on the eastern border of the Southwest.

Following the abandonment of the once densely inhabited Four Corners area, Pueblo society altered dramatically. One change was geographical. If the Pueblo Southwest is visualized as a large rectangle oriented north-south, then before 1300, Pueblo populations were clustered in its northwest quadrant, primarily on the Colorado Plateau. After 1300, however, Pueblo population was concentrated along the southern edge of the Colorado Plateau and in the basin and range country in the southeast quadrant of the rectangle. A major center developed at Casas Grandes, in the Mexican state of Chihuahua, in the southernmost corner of Pueblo territory. During this same period, large Pueblo settlements were established east of the Rio Grande, at Pecos and Las Humanas (Gran Quivira), on the edge of the grasslands inhabited by buffalo.

Large sites with congregated populations became the rule in those regions that had not been abandoned. At these large pueblos, the dramatic change in the ratio of the number of rooms to the number of kivas suggests new forms of community integration. In previous periods, a ratio of five or six rooms for each kiva was the norm. After 1325 or 1350, in most areas except the Hopi region, the ratio became 60 to 90 rooms for each kiva. This organizational change has been interpreted as a disassociation between clans and kivas, except among the Hopi, where clans continue to be key elements

136

in determining membership in kiva groups right up to the present day. Elsewhere, clans are either absent entirely or, if active, do not affect which kiva an individual joins.

At about the same time, a form of village was adopted that included plazas either partially or entirely enclosed by room blocks. With their appearance, the old Chacoan great kiva and its later derivatives, once associated with the great houses, finally disappeared. This reflects a modification in the way villages were organized, as well as in the ways in which the inhabitants of different villages related to one another.

After 1300, black-on-white painted pottery continued to be made and used in a few locations in the northern Rio Grande region; however, bichrome and polychrome wares were made throughout an enormous territory. The pottery included black-on-red and black-on-yellow types, varied by examples of black and white on red, or black and red on yellow. Much earlier, in the late 1100s and early 1200s, there had been some production of black-on-red pottery, but the vibrant polychromes, in a variety of widespread styles, were new in the late 13th and 14th centuries, and they are visually exciting. After 1325, pottery decorated with lead-based glaze paints was produced in the Rio Grande region. The glaze was never used to completely cover and waterproof ceramic vessels as it was in the Old World traditions. Rather, glaze was restricted to decorative lines.

Some of the polychrome and glaze-painted wares were made in a few locations and traded widely. Others were made in several different places but share features of style and symbol that suggest special, close relationships among the inhabitants of the settlements that produced them. Some of the design motifs painted on vessels of this period are very ancient in the Southwest. These include elements and symbols that still are recognized among the various Pueblo peoples today.

Within this period, Pueblo religion was augmented by beliefs and rituals associated with what Western Europeans refer to as katchina religion. Belief in katchinas and performance of katchina ritual are unique to the Pueblos—they occur in nearly all of the modern Pueblo villages, but not among other groups of Native Americans. In modern Pueblo belief, katchinas are divine, long-deceased ancestral beings, associated with clouds and rain. Expressing this connection, a Pueblo man stated, "The clouds are people, Pueblo people who have died, and they are rain." Today, katchina ritual includes masked dances and ceremonies. The belief system and its associated symbols, such as public performances, masks, and costumes, seem to have crystallized from disparate elements between 1300 and 1600. For the Pueblos, the katchinas provide a unifying element among villages that are different in language and in some institutions of social organization.

Finally, between 1350 and 1680, the Pueblo homeland was invaded by two groups of outsiders, events that forever changed the nature of Pueblo life.

During the late 15th and 16th centuries, the ancestors of the modern Navajo and Apache drifted south from their original homeland in central Canada and Alaska. First as hunter-gatherers, later as gardeners, traders, and raiders, and finally as pastoralists, the Athabaskan-speaking peoples eventually occupied the land between the villages of the Pueblo landscape. As one of many consequences, the kinds of contacts and relationships that had been sustained among the Pueblos themselves were altered by the presence of outsiders living between them.

Then, in 1539, the Pueblos first encountered Europeans. This contact, sporadic and of minimal impact at first, would in the end fundamentally and irrevocably change the Pueblo world. The Europeans who moved into the Pueblo realm were Spaniards, or of Spanish descent, and they had two motives: the discovery of mineral wealth for the Spanish Crown and the baptism of Indian souls for the Catholic Church. Not only were the European institutions of conquest that the invaders brought with them terribly cruel, but also some of the invaders carried them to extremes. (European courts later convicted some individuals of harsh crimes in their dealings with the Pueblos.) By 1680, these violent excesses caused the Pueblos to unite as one to kill the 21 priests and some 400 lay colonists among them, to burn all the churches, and to force the remaining survivors to march south, abandoning territory they had ruled for a century.

The massive disruptions surrounding the Conquest devastated Pueblo populations. More than 50 villages were abandoned between 1540 and 1750 alone. Two languages became extinct after the easternmost and southernmost Pueblo villages were deserted. Elsewhere, villages consolidated into fewer, larger settlements or moved to defensible landforms, or both. One group of Pueblo villages dispersed some of their population among existing settlements, while others of their people founded a village some 200 miles (321 kilometers) away. All these events had their effect on the Pueblo world from 1350 to the Spanish Colonial period, as we shall see.

Anasazi who had abandoned the Four Corners region in the 1300s had traveled south, southwest, and east, moving into territory already occupied, or at least heavily used, by other Anasazi and Mogollon. In some cases the immigrants founded new settlements. In others, they joined established villages, most likely those with which they had special ties of kinship or friendship. In the context of the gigantic regional abandonment, there must have been some degree of disorder as normal social interactions were broken and migrants moved to new and unfamiliar territories among people who—to a large extent—were strangers.

The migrants, abandoning vast areas of the Southwest, were leaving their fields and traditional hunting-and-gathering grounds, all those well-known places from which they had derived their livelihood for centuries. They were leaving their familiar households and neighbors, the graves of their ances-

Among the Pueblos, katchinas are ancestral spirits associated with rain. Katchina spirits are represented by dancers and the small carved figures the Hopi call Tihus. They are given to children and women, who do not participate in katchina ritual, as a way of sharing the blessing of these spirits. The katchina mask is the key to the identity of individual katchinas; here, a wolf katchina.

tors, and their children who had died in infancy. They were moving to new hunting territory that they would need to share with strangers. In some cases, the village itself must have been shared with outsiders. In this kind of world, beset with novel fears, any new institutions that could integrate people of heterogeneous backgrounds would be highly advantageous.

Several archaeologists infer the existence of just such integrative institutions from the symbolically rich and vividly colored painted pottery of this period, from the equally spectacular, but rare, scenes painted on the walls of kivas, and from specific, widespread, and stylistically complex rock art. Archaeologists do not always agree on the processes and new institutions, however. Some disagreements in outlook are a result of focusing on different media or regions. For example, an interpretation based on rock art may not agree with one based on pottery. For another, the distribution of ceramic types in the southern Pueblo area may suggest institutions different from those indicated by the distribution of other ceramic types in the eastern Pueblo region.

If there is one pattern that all who work on this period of adjustment recognize, it may be summed up in the word *crystallization*. Many of the specific forms, designs, symbols, and motifs from much earlier periods came together in new ways in the 14th century, forming new patterns. Similarly, architectural elements, such as rectangular kivas and plaza spaces that had wide spatial distributions and served diverse functions, become part of a new spatial vocabulary at this time.

There is little that is completely novel to this period. It is the organization of elements and their crystallization into new patterns that constitute the innovation. The effects of the abandonment of the Four Corners region before 1300 rippled throughout the still-inhabited Pueblo world. As peoples migrated into already-occupied areas, new forms of social integration and ways of interacting among villages were devised. Archaeologists have discerned four developments that coalesced as new integrative institutions between 1300 and 1600: alliance systems, a mercantile system, a Southwestern Regional Cult, and katchina ceremonies and rituals.

Archaeologist Steadman Upham proposed that among the Western Pueblos, one of the new ways in which the large aggregated villages of the 14th and 15th centuries interacted was through what he terms alliances. In his view, the large villages required a hierarchical organization of leadership in order to coordinate the labor needed to sustain themselves. In any one village, only a few individuals would be at the top of the leadership hierarchy. Upham refers to these people as elites. Alliances, therefore, were the special relationships between the elites of one community and the elites of others. Elite individuals enjoyed high status and access to special, valuable goods. The goods in turn would serve to communicate the presence of elite persons to the general population and to elites from other communities. Alliances might be reflected in the distribution of these goods at various large villages. Upham suggests that small communities did not require formal leadership hierarchies, and in any case could not sustain high-status, elite individuals. For this reason, small sites should not contain any prestige goods. Large sites would have these special items, and the abundance of these goods would correlate with the number of elites in residence. For example, Upham described what he termed the Jeddito alliance as uniting high-status or elite individuals from different sites in the ancestral Hopi area. One of the indicators of the Jeddito alliance, Upham specifies, is polychrome Jeddito Yellow ware that he finds disproportionately represented at large sites, whether or not the sites are close to its likely source of manufacture. Upham has argued that elite individuals residing at large sites had special access to these wares and that possession of the pottery signaled social interactions among these individuals.

Today, among most of the Pueblos, there is a strong egalitarian ethic. The notion of an elite class is shockingly foreign. Leaders are elders who have learned a great deal, served their people, and thus earned their respected status. Some leadership positions among the Western Pueblos are, in fact, linked by heredity to certain clans and even to families within those clans. For example, village chiefs at the Hopi Second Mesa villages are drawn traditionally from the Bear Clan. Still, leadership positions are attained by individuals from among those who are eligible. Upham's interpretation of the 14th-century Western Pueblos makes two points. One is that elite status may depend on having access to knowledge in addition to, or rather than, economic wealth. Second, he suspects that the events set in motion by the European invasion of the Southwest may have undermined a status hierarchy that had existed in the past.

Parts of the great trading center of Paquimé contained storage areas for many of the wares that were associated with the site, and pens where birds such as turkeys and macaws were bred, probably for their plumes. More than 300 scarlet macaw skeletons were recovered at the site.

Another view of the late 1200s and the 1300s also emphasizes economic and political relationships, but in a context that is not as controversial as Upham's. As we know, it was during this period that a major center developed at Casas Grandes in Chihuahua. At its height, the site contained well over 2000 habitation rooms and elaborate public buildings, including effigy mounds, ball courts, a possible market area, and a covered ditch system that may have distributed water throughout the settlement. As described by its excavator, Charles Di Peso, who directed the multiyear Joint Casas Grandes Project (a combined effort of the Amerind Foundation of the United States and the Instituto Nacional de Antropologiá e Historia of Mexico), Casas Grandes was a mercantile center. Most archaeologists, who would be reluctant to consider social hierarchies in the context of ancestral Pueblos, have little difficulty accepting the possibility of such institutions at Casas Grandes. Recent studies of burial ritual and human remains from Casas Grandes support the existence of hereditary classes.

Casas Grandes is both spectacular and spectacularly different from most Anasazi and Mogollon sites. The center and east side of the site are residential, with huge, multistory adobe house complexes. The adobe is well described in Adolph F. Bandelier's writing of nearly a century ago as a marly concrete mixed with pebbles. The timbers used in construction were squared. The western part of the site contains the ceremonial precincts, including double T-shaped ball courts, a small T-shaped ball court with subfloor burials of dismembered skeletons that suggest human sacrifice, stone-faced effigy and platform mounds, and a walk-in well and reservoir in addition to the covered ditch. Di Peso interpreted a large, open area in the center of the site as having been a market.

Di Peso concluded that Casas Grandes was a city, one that he called Paquimé, involved in the production of goods for regional and long-distance distribution. The materials he cited as part of the distribution system are scarlet macaws, turquoise, copper, shell, and pottery. More than 300 skeletons of the scarlet macaw were recovered at Casas Grandes from parts of the site that contained pens with egg shell, perches, and grain, suggesting that macaws were bred there. It is quite likely that most of the 144 skeletons recovered from other prehistoric sites in the Southwest came from Casas Grandes. Given the paucity of scarlet macaw skeletons in the Southwest in general, it is also likely that the birds were used by residents of Casas Grandes itself, perhaps for their feathers.

Turquoise is not as abundant at Casas Grandes as were other minerals. Still, almost 5 pounds (2.2 kilograms) of turquoise were recovered, mostly from rooms that Di Peso considered warehouses. Turquoise assumes somewhat greater importance in Di Peso's writings than its relative abundance might indicate, because this stone is thought to have been much valued by Mesoamerican states far to the south in central Mexico. Di Peso believed that Paquimé had been established as a mercantile outpost of one of these central Mexican states. In his later writings, Di Peso viewed Paquimé as the center of a large regional system, but one somewhat more independent of central Mexican origins.

Copper was produced in several areas of west Mexico, but Casas Grandes is the northernmost of these, yielding 32 pounds (14.6 kilograms) of copper, including 688 artifacts. These were made by a variety of techniques, including

This Ramos polychrome hooded-effigy jar, with a hollowed-out back, is of a mother with her nursing child. It was discovered whole at Rancho Corralitos, just north of Casas Grandes in Chihuahua, Mexico. While the exact purpose of this vessel is unknown, effigy forms occur in several contexts, including burials, at Casas Grandes.

Among the signals of change in 14th-century Pueblo social organization is the appearance of new, highly distinctive types of pottery, such as the Salado and Jeddito types shown here. The bright colors of the Salado Polychromes are obvious in this Tonto polychrome jar *(left)*. Archaeologist Patricia Crown suggests that the bright colors and design elements served to signal village participation in a regional religion. The distinctive Jeddito Yellow wares *(right)* of the Hopi region may reflect participation in a political alliance that united leaders or large villages, according to archaeologist Steadman Upham.

cold hammering and lost-wax casting. Copper ore was found in two rooms that may have been warehouses or work rooms. The artifacts were found in a number of contexts. Archaeologist Paul Minnis, who has collated and summarized the information from Casas Grandes, suggests that, like turquoise, copper may have been made primarily for use at Casas Grandes itself rather than for export.

Nearly 4,000,000 shell artifacts were excavated at Casas Grandes. Most of the items came from two rooms, one of which also had a large cache of copper artifacts. Di Peso inferred that the room served as a warehouse, while Minnis suggests that it might have been used by a high-status group or individual to hoard artifacts. In either case, the sheer quantity of finished shell items is impressive.

Finally, Ramos Polychrome pottery was thought to have been produced at Casas Grandes and widely traded. Compositional studies by archaeologist Anne Woosley and geochemist Bart Olinger indicate that Ramos Polychrome, probably made at Casas Grandes, was distributed to communities within a radius of about 47 miles (75 kilometers). Outside that limit, the sites with Ramos Polychrome either made the type themselves or received it from a variety of possible sources other than Casas Grandes.

Archaeologists may well debate the mercantile nature of Casas Grandes for years. They will certainly learn more about the ways in which resources were procured at Casas and distributed beyond the site. In the present con-

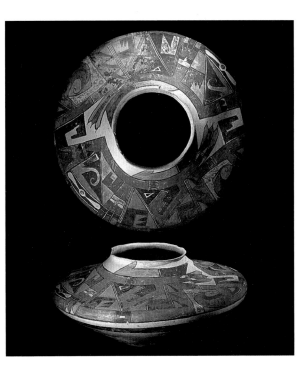

Late 14th- and 15th-century pottery from the Mogollon Rim area of central Arizona included types such as Four Mile polychrome *(left)*. The colors and bold designs owe much to their Mogollon ancestry, and were widely traded and widely imitated. Fifteenth-century Hopi Sikyatki polychrome *(right)* links the late prehistoric and historic Hopi. The superbly executed and complicated design elements are symbols that were widespread in prehistoric times and that are recognized by Pueblo peoples today. This style was revived by the famous Hopi potter Mampeyo at the turn of the 20th century.

text, it is of interest that Casas Grandes developed as an enormous and significant center, whose influence derived from its economic and political status. It is not thought to be the source of any of the religious-belief systems that are believed to have been integrating forces among refugees from recently abandoned districts to the north.

According to Patricia Crown, an archaeologist at the University of New Mexico, what she calls the Southwestern Regional Cult originated among Kayenta Anasazi migrants who joined Mogollon populations in the Mogollon Rim area of Arizona between A.D. 1280 and 1300, and quickly spread over an enormous area that includes the Hopi and White Mountain regions as well as the Rio Grande. Her analysis initially focused on painted ceramic types collectively known as the Salado Polychromes that were made in the Mogollon Rim country. The earliest of the Salado Polychromes is decorated in a style called Pinedale that is characterized by a series of distinctive images and symbols.

The Southwestern Regional Cult is recognizable through a series of images found in the Pinedale style that Crown suggests make up an iconic system. The images include parrots, snakes, horned serpents, eyes, the sun, and stars. As a system, these icons appear on pottery and other media, such as rock art, and have meanings Crown relates to water control and fertility. Both the icons and the meanings are quite general, occurring in Mesoamerican and historic Pueblo religions.

In the Southwest, the icons painted on pottery appear as early as Classic Mimbres pottery dating to the 1000s. While all the Southwestern Regional Cult icons may be found on Mimbres pottery, the reverse is not true. Many symbols and other unusual paintings occur only on Mimbres pottery. In addition, the contexts in which Mimbres and later cult pottery are found are very different. When Mimbres bowls occur in burials, they are part of standard burial patterns that suggest a single ritual. The later cult pottery is found in a variety of burial modes. The earlier Mimbres pottery is associated with long-lived settlements, and in fact is found with the in-place development of above-ground pueblos from pit-house communities. The later Southwestern Regional Cult pottery is found at many newly established villages. Crown believes that an argument could be made for the Mimbres representations being part of ancestor worship. This is not true of the later Southwestern Regional Cult. She maintains that the imagery of the Mimbres area was used for many centuries in the Southwest, and that it crystallized in the Southwestern Regional Cult in the late 13th century.

Crown describes the Southwestern Regional Cult as comparable to similar belief systems known for Africa and elsewhere. Regional cults are neither the ancestor cults or other kin-based religions common in tribes, nor "universal" world religions, such as Catholicism or Buddhism. Regional cults emphasize shared values and concern with the earth and fertility, and tend to develop during times of social disruption. They can unify people of diverse backgrounds. The cult could have co-existed with several different, perhaps local, ideologies. The Southwestern Regional Cult not only includes aspects of katchina beliefs, but also traces of other religious systems in Mexico and the U.S. Southwest. Such a regional religion might well have been highly advantageous among the ethnically heterogeneous villagers of the post-abandonment Southwest.

Based on his experience excavating historic and ancestral Hopi villages, archaeologist E. Charles Adams of the Arizona State Museum argues that katchina rituals, specifically, developed as an institution of social integration among Mogollon and Anasazi villages in the Upper Little Colorado region in the 15th century. He views the beginning of katchina beliefs as being slightly later than, and occurring to the northeast of, Crown's suggested origination of the Southwestern Regional Cult. The Upper Little Colorado area was for centuries at a cultural boundary between the Mogollon and Anasazi traditions. It was also a major area of refuge for people moving south out of the Four Corners region.

Among the Pueblos, katchinas serve as mediators between humans and gods, bringing the people's needs for rain and crop fertility to the attention of the gods. They are also generalized ancestral beings, in that certain of the dead are believed to become katchinas. Katchina ceremonies are nearly universal in the pueblos but are most apparent today among the Western Pueblo

Hopi dancers perform at a ceremony in which the katchina spirits are impersonated by initiated men who become katchinas themselves when they dance with masks, which they call "friends." This photograph was taken in 1901 at Shongopavi Pueblo, Arizona Territory. Nowadays, the Hopi are very reluctant to have their ceremonies photographed.

villages of the Hopi, Zuni, and Acoma. Among the Rio Grande Pueblos, the public aspects of katchina ritual became private and secret in response to Spanish repression of Native religion. Among the Western Pueblos, katchina dances are performed in the central plaza before a spectator audience. During these ceremonies, the katchina spirits are impersonated by initiated men who become katchinas themselves by dancing with objects that they call friends and Western Europeans call masks. The katchina rituals involve elaborate costumes and dancing that reflect long periods of planning and preparation. The public katchina performances involve cooperation among the various clans or kiva groups of the Pueblo villages. Adams views these aspects of the katchina religion as requiring the kind of cooperation that cuts across households and clans.

In Western Pueblo society, male clan elders are the village leaders. There are also two classes of katchinas, chief katchinas and dancing katchinas; the distinction mirrors that between clan elders and other initiated males in Western Pueblo society. The katchina cult thus serves to institutionalize aspects of Western Pueblo social and political organization. In Adams's view, the qualities of cooperation among residence and kin groups, as well as the reflection of the Western Pueblo organizational features, were likely forces

145

for integrating villages formed by the heterogeneous elements in the wake of the abandonments of the late 13th century.

It is difficult to learn from the archaeological record when and where the katchina belief system began, because this would require specific material manifestation of katchina beliefs. Adams describes such symbols as the masks themselves, the group performance and its setting in a plaza, the kiva where dances are planned and practiced, private rest areas used between specific performances, and preparation and distribution of specific kinds of food, especially the wafer-thin corn bread called *piki* that the Hopi make.

The masks that are the key features of katchinas today are unlikely to become part of the archaeological record, or to be preserved. It is no surprise that no katchina masks have been found in archaeological context. Some katchina cult symbols, such as lightning, snake designs, or the terraced cloud motif, are very ancient examples of Pueblo symbolism, and are older and more widespread geographically than are katchina beliefs. Other elements such as rectangular kivas are not functionally specific to the cult, but serve a variety of uses. Nevertheless, Adams maintains that the principal features of the katchina rituals are village plans with enclosed plazas, rectangular kivas, and griddle stones for making piki bread, and that these came together in the 1300s in the Upper Little Colorado River area. The spread of the katchina beliefs can be identified archaeologically by the symbols on ceramics, kiva wall murals, and, in the Rio Grande area, in rock art.

In Adams's view, an important aspect in the development and spread of Katchina rituals was for villages to publicly indicate that they participated in the ceremonies. In the Upper Little Colorado and the Hopi areas, the signal involved pictorial representations of masks, masked figures, and other katchina symbols painted on pottery and in murals on the walls of rectangular kivas. These forms of representation also spread to the east and are found at Pottery Mound and at Kuaua, large villages in the Rio Grande area, and at Abó, Quarai, and Las Humanas (Gran Quivira) on the edge of the Plains.

The pottery style that is most closely associated with katchina depiction is named Four Mile, after the type site in the White Mountains of Arizona. Four Mile pottery is generally considered to have developed from older Kayenta ceramic types and in turn to be ancestral to later Hopi polychrome types. In this interpretation of the language of pottery, the Tsegi-phase Kayenta Anasazi continued to produce distinctive pottery after they had abandoned their canyon homelands. The katchina belief system was accepted by descendants of these Kayenta Anasazi and by other Anasazi and Mogollon peoples among whom they lived in the large aggregated villages of the 14th century.

Art historian Helen Crotty writes that painting the walls of kivas is an ancient practice in Anasazi prehistory. It is not until the late 14th and 15th centuries, however, that such painting depicts masked figures. Once again,

This reproduction of a late 15th- or early 16th-century kiva mural from the archaeological site of Kuaua, a pueblo in central New Mexico, has been interpreted by Pueblo people as the Universe with a figure called Lightning Man. In this universe, the ordinary laws of nature are suspended. Fish and birds spit seed and water in the sky. Such murals were produced on walls with many layers of plaster, not all of which were painted. The elaborate religious ritual and rich symbols of this period reveal the importance of religion as a means of integrating the large settlements that may have included "refugees" from various regions after the abandonments of the late 13th century.

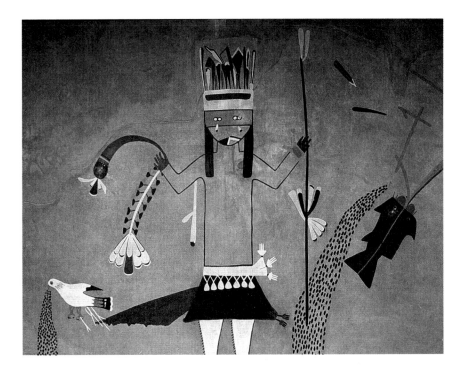

this time in the context of katchina beliefs, older, diverse elements crystallize into something new. Finding kiva murals is a rare event in southwestern archaeology. Murals depicting katchinas are known from Awatovi, Kawaika-a, Pottery Mound, and Kuaua. Katchina figures also occurred in square rooms, not kivas, at Las Humanas.

While it is unlikely that these sites are exactly contemporary, they share technical methods of execution, plan, and symbols. The murals depict single figures, altars, and scenes that include masked dancers. Kiva murals were produced on walls with multiple layers of plaster. For example, one wall at Kuaua had 85 layers of plaster, of which 17 were painted. The precise way in which the murals were integrated into ceremonies is not known. However, because paintings were plastered over and some were literally "defaced" by having the face chipped or broken off prehistorically, presumably it was the act of making the paintings, rather than subsequently viewing them, that was important. Another explanation is that such defacing may have been a ritual substitute for human sacrifice.

The Rio Grande style of rock art, especially as represented in the Galisteo Basin south of Santa Fe, incorporates masks and masked figures. This style has been described as descended from the Jornada Mogollon style of rock art known from the eastern and southern periphery of Pueblo country, and has been interpreted as indicating a southern origin of the katchina cult. However, Crotty notes that the mask forms in Jornada rock art are completely different in style from those on pottery and kiva murals. She suggests that this argues for much greater antiquity of the use of masks than is normally credited, and she agrees with Adams that those representing the presence of katchina beliefs are from the west.

As with the Southwestern Regional Cult, the katchina religion seems to have crystallized out of diverse and very ancient elements in Pueblo culture. The beliefs and rituals successfully integrated Pueblo peoples of different languages and histories. They were particularly successful at times of population movement and concomitant social stress. The late 16th and early 17th centuries were also a time of movement and distress as Athabaskan-speaking peoples moved into the Southwest. These newcomers never were integrated into the Pueblo social world, but there are intriguing suggestions that they might have been, had historical circumstances been different.

Today, the closest neighbors of many of the Pueblos are the Navajo and Apache, who moved into the Southwest from their subarctic homeland. The Navajo have the highest rate of population growth of any North American Native Americans. Despite the current numerical prominence of these people, archaeologists have not identified the route or routes over which they entered the Southwest, nor have they agreed about precisely when these people did so. Indeed, part of the problem is the difficulty in knowing what to look for, because when they entered the Southwest, the Athabaskan-speaking peoples were mobile hunters and gatherers whose artifactual remains were very thinly scattered over the region and consisted primarily of stone tools of generalized types and a limited amount of unpainted gray pottery. Temporary brush structures were most often the only kinds of housing they made. The ancestors of the Navajo who lived in the Upper San Juan area of New Mexico very quickly adopted corn cultivation from the Pueblos, and, along with it, the manos and metates for processing the dried grain. The earliest radiocarbon dates for Navajo sites are from sites in this area with temporary shelters, gray utility ware, corn, and manos and metates that have been dated to A.D. 1500.

There is no archaeological documentation relevant to understanding the ways that Navajo, Apache, and Pueblos interacted initially in the 1500s. Over most of the later historic periods, from the 1830s on, Pueblos and Athabaskan speakers were uneasy neighbors, and indeed often were enemies. This state of affairs is attributable to their competing for the resources of land, water, and, later, mineral rights in the wake of European colonization. Long before then, there was close interaction between Pueblo and Navajo that is reflected in substantial Pueblo influence on Navajo culture. As mentioned, the Navajo adopted maize cultivation, where there was suitable land, and the tools Pueblos traditionally used to process corn. In addition, some aspects of Navajo religion, specifically dealing with divine supernaturals called *yei*, owe some of their inspiration to the katchina. In the historic peri-

During the period following the Spanish Reconquest, the Navajo, fearing acts of reprisal, built fortified stone dwellings called pueblitos in highly defensive and inaccessible locations such as this one in northwestern New Mexico.

od, after the introduction of sheep by the Europeans, the Navajo became justifiably world-famous as weavers, a skill they had learned from the Pueblos.

During the period from A.D. 1690 to 1780, Navajo and Pueblo interactions were particularly close. At the time of the Pueblo Revolt of 1680 and the reconquest of 1692-93, both Pueblo and Navajo feared acts of revenge by the Spanish. The Navajo built stone dwellings, called pueblitos, in highly defensive and inaccessible locations. Pueblitos resemble Pueblo architecture, and, despite the use of the diminutive term in the name, they vary considerably in size, some being quite large. Navajos also made a pottery type called Gobernador Polychrome that greatly resembles Pueblo pottery of the time. In fact, the pottery provides some insight into the nature of Pueblo-Navajo relations during this dangerous time.

Spanish documents indicate that at the time of the reconquest, the Pueblos were moving out of their traditional territory in fear of reprisals. Many of the Pueblo residents of the Galisteo Basin abandoned their homes as did people from Santa Clara, San Ildefonso, Jemez, and Pojoaque. Most of these Pueblos sought refuge among the Acoma, Zuni, and Hopi. The best-known example is the establishment of the villages of Hopi-Tewa or Hano and Polacca at the Hopi First Mesa by Tano-speakers from the Galisteo Basin pueblos of San Lazaro and San Cristobal. The villages at

Hopi are inhabited by their descendants today. Less well-known is that some Pueblos took refuge with the Navajo.

Archaeologists Lori Stephens Reed and Paul F. Reed have explored the evidence for Pueblo-Navajo interaction in terms of exchanges of goods and information. They find that there are Pueblo trade ceramics found on Navajo sites that date from before 1680, the amount of which is very limited but includes examples of Western Pueblo and Rio Grande wares. These are important in establishing the existence of trade between the two peoples at an early date. Obsidian that comes from sources in the Jemez Mountains also appears on Navajo sites at this early time, and most probably was an additional item of trade from the Pueblos.

In their examination of Gobernador Polychrome, the Reeds note that as a yellow ware, the type represents a continuation of the yellow-ware tradition of the Hopi and the Rio Grande villages, and they suggest that the Navajo who made it were using the language of pottery as used by the Pueblos to signal a social affiliation with Pueblo groups. The Reeds have found a number of intriguing cases in which Gobernador Polychrome dates prior to the Pueblo Revolt. They suggest that when those Pueblo did seek refuge among the Navajo, they were accepted in large part because there was a well-established alliance between the two peoples that had grown out of relationships of long-standing trade and social interaction. It is fascinating but futile to wonder what kinds of relationships might have developed between Pueblos and Navajos over the centuries had not the Southwest finally been conquered by Europeans.

The beginning of that conquest occurred between 1528 and 1539, when survivors of a Spanish shipwreck off the coast of Texas marched inland, eventually meeting up with their countrymen in what today is Sonora, Mexico. The survivors reported learning of wealthy agricultural villages to the north on the Rio Grande. This information was the stimulus for two expeditions—one in 1539 that was terminated at Zuni, where the "scout" was killed; the second from 1540 to 1542. The latter was a well-financed and well-organized expedition under the leadership of Francisco Vásquez de Coronado.

The expedition led by Coronado consisted of 300 soldiers, 6 Franciscan friars, hundreds of Mexican Indians, 1000 horses, and 600 pack animals. The campaign reached Hawikuh on July 7, 1540. Some of the forces explored the Hopi villages, others went on to the Grand Canyon. With his main army, Coronado marched to the Tiguex Pueblos on the Rio Grande, camping at modern Bernalillo, New Mexico, during late 1540 and early 1541. In the spring they explored as far north as Pecos before returning to Mexico. Coronado was tremendously disappointed by the lack of mineral wealth among the Pueblos. He left two friars among them, but they were killed. It would be 40 years before another Spanish expedition ventured into the Southwest. The hiatus in exploration was most likely the result of the discovery of silver in Zacatecas, Mexico. Forty years is not a great length of time, but it amounts to two generations. From the perspective of the Pueblos, it must have seemed a lengthy reprieve. In 1598, Juan de Oñate, along with 400 soldiers, colonists, friars, and Mexican Indians, entered the Rio Grande Valley with the object of founding a colony and establishing missions among the Pueblos. Oñate extracted pledges of loyalty from the Pueblos, declared New Mexico a missionary province, and established a settlement at San Gabriel del Yunque at modern San Juan Pueblo. The reprieve had come to an end.

Because New Mexico lacked great mineral wealth, the colonial effort of the 1600s was focused on "missionizing" the Pueblos. The Pueblos were forced to build the governor's palace and other administrative buildings in Santa Fe and about 40 mission churches throughout the colony. The scale of this effort is astonishing. A single mission excavated by 20th-century archaeologists consisted of many rooms around a cloister or sacred garden, a group of offices and schoolrooms, three churches—two more than 100 feet long—and the foundations of barracks for a military garrison. Before 1680, Native American labor to construct the missions could be obtained legally by force.

Under Spanish law, traditional Native religious practices were prohibited, dances forbidden, sacred objects destroyed, and individuals discovered committing acts of idolatry were killed. Not only were the Native Americans required to provide labor to build the missions, they were forced to cultivate mission lands, care for mission herds and flocks, and to work in sweatshops weaving, smithing, painting, and providing other services. Among the most detested of the Spanish laws were those of the *repartimiento* and the *encomienda*. The repartimiento forced the Pueblos to provide labor for Spanish farms, households, and mining activities. The encomienda required the Pueblos to provide tribute in the form of produce and goods. Although the Spaniards introduced livestock to the Pueblos, new crops—principally wheat and fruit trees—and crafts such as smithing and silverworking, the benefits, as a whole, were few.

A chief complaint among the Pueblos was that they had little time to care for their own fields or to protect their own homes from increasingly devastating Apache raids. The trade relationships between Pueblo and Apache had been disrupted because the Pueblos did not have the labor or time to produce the surpluses they needed to trade for the hides and meat they were legally required to give as tribute to the Spaniards. Meanwhile, the Apache had acquired horses from the Spaniards, giving them an advantage in striking they had not had before. In 1673, for example, an Apache raid on the Zuni Pueblo of Hawikuh killed the priest and 200 Zuni. One thousand Zuni were captured, all the livestock taken, and the village burned. Finally, on August 10, 1680, the Pueblos carried out their well-organized, planned revolt and succeeded, albeit temporarily, in removing the Spaniards from their midst.

The tiny village of Taos Pueblo still retains the flavor of a prehistoric pueblo. Its multistoried dwellings are made entirely of adobe, the main story is set back about 15 feet (4.5 meters) from the floor below it; wooden ladders provide access to the upper levels. Taos is home to about

9

PUEBLO LEGACIES: CONTINUITY AND CHANGE

Taken together, European history, traditional Pueblo history, and archaeology provide a richer contextual picture of the Spanish Mission and Colonial periods than can be glimpsed from any one source alone.

An unusually productive view of the Spanish conquest comes from the Hopi villages. Although the Spanish impact was less intensive among the Hopi and Zuni than among the other Pueblo villages, the historic record of this period at Hopi is bolstered by archaeological information

buildings rising to a height of five stories. Each 2500 Pueblo people.

The impact of the Spanish conquest on the Pueblos has been documented through important excavations at the Hopi pueblos of Awatovi and Walpi, and at Pecos and Gran Quivira in New Mexico. The inter-relationships between the Pueblos and the Plains tribes are also evident at Pecos and Gran Quivira.

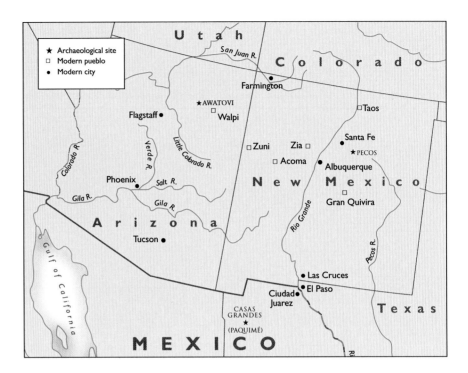

that is missing elsewhere. When Francisco Vásquez de Coronado stopped at Zuni in 1540, he dispatched some of his party to Hopi. They were led by a general, Pedro de Tovar, and a Franciscan friar, Juan de Padilla. It was not until 1629, however, that missions were established at the Hopi villages. Eventually, 17th-century mission churches were built at Awatovi, at that time the easternmost Hopi village on Antelope Mesa; at Shongopavi, on Second Mesa; and at Oraibi, on Third Mesa.

At Awatovi—the site of San Bernardo, the largest mission church—we have traditional Hopi history, official accounts of the Spanish chroniclers, and archaeological remains. Here the Spaniards directed that the mission church be built directly over the principal kiva and that all Native religious objects be surrendered and destroyed. At the time, the villagers at Awatovi seem to have complied, not unwillingly, with most of the Spaniards' requests. Nevertheless, during the Pueblo Revolt of 1680, the mission church of San Bernardo de Awatovi was destroyed. In August of 1692 Diego de Vargas led a military expedition into New Mexico demanding allegiance of the Pueblo villages. On September 14, 1692, during a momentary lull in the fighting, Vargas announced the Spanish repossession of Santa Fe and the Pueblo world while the Franciscan brothers absolved the Pueblos of their apostasy. In fact, the Spanish Reconquest was far from complete, and fighting continued off and on throughout the 17th century. During this turbulent Reconquest period, the village of Awatovi was destroyed by Hopi from other villages.

In the 1890s, small-scale excavations were made at Awatovi by J. W. Fewkes on behalf of the Smithsonian Institution. During the 1930s, archaeologists working under J. O. Brew, from Harvard University's Peabody Museum, conducted major work at the same site, including complete excavation of the mission church of San Bernardo.

A detailed, though different, record is available for the First Mesa Hopi village of Walpi. Walpi was established at its current mesatop location in 1690, after the Pueblo Revolt, and continues to be inhabited today. There are traditional Hopi histories and brief Spanish chronicle notes on Walpi, as well as ethnographic and United States Government records. Between 1975 and 1977, Walpi commissioned archaeological work, conducted under the direction of E. Charles Adams, in conjunction with a village restoration project. The archaeology again provided an additional reservoir of data.

The uniquely rich mine of information from both the Awatovi and Walpi sources can be touched upon only lightly here. As a whole, it enhances the picture we have of Hopi rejection of the Spaniards and some of the material results of the physical disruptions the Hopi sustained during the post-contact period.

The Spanish missionization at Awatovi was their most successful among the Hopi. According to the Spanish documentary record, a miraculous cure of a blind Hopi boy by the Franciscan friar Francisco Porras, in 1629, was behind this success. Whether or not such an event actually occurred, the missionary achievements can be attributed, in part, to the character of Porras himself, who was an outstanding churchman of his times. He was responsible for building the magnificent mission church of San Bernardo and baptizing many Awatovi. He also is said to have learned the Hopi language.

The Hopi villages, however, participated enthusiastically in the Revolt of 1680. The four then-resident clerics were killed and the missions destroyed. As there were no European survivors of the revolt, and documents were burned, there are no contemporary written accounts of the actual events. The archaeological excavations demonstrate that San Bernardo was indeed burned. Subsequently, the people of Awatovi remodeled the friary and occupied it as part of the pueblo.

At Hopi, the events of 1680 marked the end for the Spaniards' church and their Christian God. It was a victory for the katchinas in all the villages and the victory was sustained. The Hopi never again were administered successfully as a part of the Spanish Empire. Yet, for their own reasons, the Awatovi people continued to bury Christian Hopi at the burned mission, and in contrast to all the rest of the Hopi pueblos, were prepared to invite the Spaniards to return in 1700. But other Hopi refused to permit them to do so.

According to a later Spanish account (of 1732), two Franciscan friars traveled to Hopi in 1700. At Awatovi they successfully converted the Pueblos, baptizing many. During their stay, they were threatened by Pueblos from other Hopi vil-

lages, whom they tried, unsuccessfully, to convert. Intending to return with soldiers to protect the new Christians of Awatovi, they departed. After they had gone, Hopi warriors from several other villages raided, sacked, and destroyed Awatovi.

According to traditional Hopi history, historical accounts, and the archaeological evidence, the entire village of Awatovi was burned; many of its men were killed, and captives were taken to the other villages. Fewkes recorded an addition to the Hopi account. He learned from the Hopi that on the way back to the other villages, several of the captives were killed, dismembered, and mutilated.

Archaeology supplements these accounts by revealing information that makes the attack on Awatovi understandable, and by corroborating the Hopi version of events. The friars who came to Awatovi were after more than converts. They asked the Awatovi to build a barracks that would serve as a staging area from which to reconquer the other villages. Clear evidence that the Awatovi had complied with the request came during the 1930s when the foundations of the barracks were excavated. The return of the Spaniards to Awatovi was, therefore, a very real threat to the rest of the Hopi.

In 1964, the skeletal remains of more than 30 individuals, of both sexes and all ages, were excavated at a mass burial site at Polacca Wash, about 4 miles (6.5 kilometers) from the Hopi villages. The bones were of individuals of Western Pueblo physical type. They had been mutilated violently at the grave site, battered by multiple splintering, fracturing blows while still alive. Some individuals seem to have been cannibalized. Radiocarbon dates place the grave site in the historic period. The site's evidence confirms the Hopi traditional history that had been related to Fewkes.

While the Hopi rejected the Spanish friars, their religious and government institutions, they did assimilate those things they considered useful: metal plows and hoes for farming; the cultivation of melons, apples, peaches, and apricots; mutton and chicken; methods of weaving with wool, new ways of working wood, and skill in crafting metal tools.

Hopi pottery dating to this mission period includes European forms such as shallow, flare-rimmed stew bowls and bowls with a single coil affixed to the base, replicating the ring-base of European wheel-made pottery. In addition, the Pueblos used various European motifs in painted designs on these and more traditional forms made between 1630 and 1680.

The village of Walpi was founded in 1690, 10 years after the successful Pueblo Revolt. Between that date and the 1730s, the population of all the Hopi villages, including Walpi, swelled as refugees from the Rio Grande villages tried to escape as far as possible from the threat of Spanish reprisals after the revolt. The excavations at Walpi provide data that reflect the very strong anti-Spanish feelings. All European vessel forms and Spanish design motifs disappear from the Hopi pottery. The forms of bowls and jars and the designs used are similar to the Rio Grande pottery of the period, a fact that seems to reflect the refugee elements in the Hopi communities and the close ties the Hopi established with these people.

Droughts at Hopi during the 1730s spurred many Rio Grande Pueblo refugees to begin returning home. Tano people from the Galisteo Basin stayed, however, and founded Hano, a First Mesa village that is still occupied by their descendants today. After 1750, anti-Spanish feeling abated somewhat, and, according to Adams, Spanish elements once again appear on Hopi pottery. Their form, overall organization, and motifs, however, are a mixture of Spanish, Hopi, and Rio Grande design.

Tragedy struck the Hopi again, when a major drought occurred between 1777 and 1780, followed by a smallpox epidemic that swept through the Hopi villages in 1781. In response to these events, a number of Hopi families temporarily moved to Zuni, Acoma, Zia, and other pueblos where they had friends or relatives. When the drought ended and the Hopi returned to their villages, the pottery they subsequently produced was much changed. The unslipped light yellow, tan, or orange pottery that had been made previously was replaced by pottery with white slips that resembled Zuni and Acoma pottery. Spanish forms, such as stew bowls, and Spanish design elements again became popular. Adams indicates that these were assimilated indirectly by the Hopi through their acculturated friends at other villages. This kind of pottery continued to be made into the American period until it was replaced by Hopi "revival" pottery.

A less detailed and generally quite different scenario of the effects of Spanish and Pueblo interaction is available from Pecos and Las Humanas (Gran Quivira) at the extreme eastern edge of the Pueblo world. Here, the groups involved included nomadic Apache and the Comanche from the Plains in addition to Pueblos and Spaniards. The official Spanish Colonial documents and the letters of colonists are supplemented by archaeological work of Alfred Kidder at Pecos, R. Gwinn Vivian and Alden Hayes, and most recently Katherine Spielmann at Las Humanas, and by John Speth at protohistoric sites on the extreme western edge of the southern Great Plains. In addition, Judith Habicht-Mauche contributes an important study of some of the material culture of the protohistoric southern Plains groups. The rich documentary history of Pecos has been synthesized by historian John Kessell, but only the most cursory sketch of this work can be given here.

In the 14th and 15th centuries, a convergence of processes affecting the Rio Grande area and the southern Plains brought about well-developed interactions among groups of both areas. The Pueblo farmers of the Rio Grande experienced increasing climatic deterioration at the same time that their population was swollen by refugees from the Four Corners. Concurrently, the Plains margins that for centuries had been occupied by hunter-gatherers came to be inhabited by new groups who, while still nomadic, were more specialized bison hunters.

A mantle of snow cloaks the Hopi village of Walpi, atop First Mesa. The village, little altered since its founding in 1690, is still inhabited today. Telephone poles and a pickup truck, parked in someone's yard, are reminders of the pueblo's present-day occupants.

Whenever they could, the Pueblos of Pecos and Las Humanas planted enough corn to ensure a surplus, their goal being a storage capacity of two years. Spielmann states that an economy based on mutually beneficial exchange developed between Pueblos and Plains groups in the mid-15th and 16th centuries. Pecos and Las Humanas, the eastern border pueblos, became centers of contact between Pueblos and Plains. They received both Pueblo and Plains products and transferred goods between the two areas. Bison hides and meat moved west from Pecos and Las Humanas. Corn, pottery, obsidian, and turquoise moved east. The historic record documents annual trade fairs that took place at Pecos when seminomadic Plains hunters camped at the pueblo for several weeks while engaged in exchange. Kidder's excavations at Pecos yielded Plains-manufactured items such as knives made of Alibates flint from Texas and Apache ceramics.

The trade, however, was more than a reciprocal exchange of material goods. Studies by Judith Habicht-Mauche show that between 1500 and 1700, southern Plains groups not only accepted Rio Grande Pueblo-made glaze-decorated pottery but were producing their own version of Pueblo unpainted cooking and storage ware. Finding such vessels on sites far to the east of the Pecos River, in camping places used by seminomadic hunters, reflects the existence of intensive relations between Pueblo and Plains peoples. Habicht-

The partially reconstructed mission church stands behind a kiva at Pecos Pueblo. As part of the Spanish colonial effort, Spanish Franciscans demanded the Native American labor that built the imposing mission church and convent here in 1622. After years of hardship and injustice, the Pueblos united, and on August 10, 1680, began a revolt that drove the Spanish from their world. At Pecos, the mission and convent were burned. In an attempt to return to their old ways, the Pueblos constructed their kiva on the site of the razed convent.

Mauche maintains that the cooking pottery demonstrates that a tradition of food-preparation and the technology associated with it were disseminated. For this to have happened, interactions must have been very close, possibly involving intermarriage.

The first Spanish capital established in 1598 at San Gabriel del Yunque at the confluence of the Rio Chama and the Rio Grande at San Juan Pueblo and the second capital, built in 1610 at Santa Fe, were much closer to the Rio Grande Pueblos than other Spanish administrative centers were to Hopi. Further, Hispanic colonists established themselves in the Rio Grande Valley, whereas there were no Spanish Colonial villages in the vicinity of the Hopi. The proximity of the Spaniards and Pueblos allowed the Spaniards to directly tax the Rio Grande Pueblos for labor and tribute. At the same time, the more nomadic Plains tribes came to demand European products such as horses, guns, and iron tools.

160

In the 1400s, villages in the Rio Grande area and as far east as Pecos and Gran Quivira reorganized in response to increased migration from the Mesa Verde and northern San Juan area. New centers of trade arose, as well as new regional pottery styles. Along the Rio Chama and north of Santa Fe, a type known as biscuit ware (*top left*)—because it resembles European pottery fired to the biscuit stage—was made and widely traded. South of Santa Fe and east to Pecos and the Great Plains, Pueblo potters decorated bowls and jars with a black glaze paint (*top right*), produced by adding galena (lead) to a flux. The bowl shown here displays the classic Pueblo motif—the *awanyu,* or feathered serpent.

The pre-revolt Spanish tax on Pueblo labor and the demand of the Spanish Empire for tribute in corn, hides, and tallow disrupted the ongoing exchange between Pueblos and Plains peoples. Pueblos could not produce enough to feed themselves, pay tribute to the Spaniards, and maintain their obligations to trade with their neighbors on the Plains. Further, the Spaniards themselves began to trade with the Plains groups. One of the changes that seems to have occurred as a result was the development among the Pueblos of factionalized communities and an incipient class system composed of high-status leaders who set themselves apart from everyone else. The leaders acted as middlemen for the Spaniards both in collecting tribute and coordinating the trade of Pueblo goods for Plains' products. As long as tribute was paid and trade maintained, they were able to enrich themselves to some degree at the expense of their own communities and the Spaniards. When there were agricultural shortfalls and the Pueblos could not meet their trade obligations, the situation deteriorated into armed conflict between Pueblo and Plains groups, especially the Comanche. After the reconquest, this raiding and warfare contributed significantly to eventual abandonment of Pecos, Las Humanas, and other eastern margin villages.

Spanish documents report that Colonial governors dealt only with specific leaders or headmen among the Pueblos. Sometimes, these individuals were provided with goods to exchange with the Plains peoples. At the time of the revolt, the leaders at Pecos and among the Galisteo Basin Pueblos were not interested in taking part, although the general populace did participate. At least some of the disorder and internal fighting that characterized the period between 1680 and the beginning of the Spanish reconquest in 1692 stems from this insidious factionalism.

The changes European conquest wrought on the Pueblos cannot be overestimated. At the most basic level, European diseases, such as smallpox, drastically reduced their numbers. The death toll was also increased by over-taxing Pueblo labor and taking food from the villages by force, and through the internecine conflict among Pueblos, Apache, and Comanche. While the Europeans did introduce new crops and domestic animals to supplement the dogs and turkeys already possessed by the Pueblos, European livestock changed the character of the native vegetation. Familiar gathered foods, foods that might have made the difference between survival and starvation when maize crops were poor, no longer grew in abundance in the altered habitat.

For centuries, the Pueblos had been able to adjust subsistence problems, at least in part, by moving to new territory. The Spaniards precluded this strategy in two ways. By law, Spanish settlements were to be established outside existing pueblos. While there were many infractions of the law and encroachments on Pueblo lands, those legally established colonial settlements occupied territory that was then off limits for Pueblo settlement. Second, by occupying the lands between villages and by outlawing short- and long-term migrations, the Spaniards so disrupted relationships among the different Pueblo villages themselves that it became very difficult for one village or group of villages to serve as places of refuge for others.

With their numbers greatly reduced, an imposed religion, and a similarly inflicted European legal system, the acceptance of new food sources and novel forms of transportation, it is logical to ask to what extent Pueblo culture today reflects its traditional past. Clearly, change must be acknowledged. Nevertheless, remarkable continuity in Pueblo culture has been sustained. For example, Pueblo people today learn their ancient languages in addition to English, and often Spanish. Pueblo religious institutions, many of them secret, remain remarkably intact, as do the internal, traditional structures of government. Value systems, kinship organization, and ancient patterns of interaction with outsiders have also been retained.

Among Pueblo men and women today, there are administrators, anthropologists, artists, doctors, educators, engineers, foresters, historians, journalists, lawyers, linguists, merchants, museum curators, nurses, professors, secretaries, writers, and others who contribute to society through their occupations and daily interactions with other Americans. Some of these people can continue to live in their traditional communities and commute to work. Others return home on weekends and feast days in order to visit and participate in community events and ceremonies. Whether or not the traditional Pueblo ways were in danger of dying out in the 1950s, as some maintained, they blossomed from the late 1960s on, when participation became a matter of ethnic pride.

From the late 1960s, the Pueblo, like other Native Americans, came to symbolize the values of American counterculture. Their philosophy and ways of life were to be emulated by many young Americans. Unlike so many Native Americans who live in rural or urban poverty, where the landscape has no features with names in their native language, the Pueblos inhabit their ancient homeland, living in villages that have existed for centuries. They have names for the mountains, springs, and rivers in their native tongues. They know when and where to gather traditional medicinal herbs and have the resources to make tools. They know where their forebears lie buried and which among the countless ruined villages of the past are those once occupied by their village or clan ancestors during the migrations.

Both continuity and change link the Pueblos of the past to their modern descendants. Continuity of language, religious beliefs, and community organization is a particularly strong element of Pueblo culture. But for the archaeologist—and for tourists, visitors, and other Americans who live in the Southwest—perhaps the most relevant elements of the culture are those that are most durable. And of these, none are more obvious or central than traditional architecture and pottery.

Few who visit Chaco Canyon or Mesa Verde come away without being impressed by the multistory great houses and cliff dwellings. Visits to many of the pueblos that are occupied today, vibrant with all the activity of daily life, allow outsiders to experience the kind of living spaces that are only hinted at in the archaeological sites.

The pueblo dwelling form is unusual in worldwide vernacular architecture. It is a form in which the village as a community of people who interact daily and as an architectural unit are one and the same. Today's travel writers sometimes refer to pueblos as apartment houses, but nothing could be less descriptive. In contrast to the atomized, space-saving, urban high-rise, the pueblo is a social unit. While individual families do have private household space, the plazas and kivas are communal areas of daily use. Occupants of the same pueblo not only speak a common language and have their own internal government (one that today includes tribal constitutions and tribal police), but they have known one another and their families all of their lives. They are encouraged to marry within the community and to share the same standards of ethical conduct. Socially, pueblos resemble villages throughout the world.

The archaeological record demonstrates that pithouses were the first forms of semipermanent residential architecture, used in both the Mogollon and Anasazi areas. The transition to above-ground dwellings with contiguous rooms also occurred in both areas. Among the Anasazi, the change occurred at about A.D. 750. Among the Mogollon it seems to have been slightly later, at about A.D. 900 or 950. Among the Anasazi, where the change seems to have been somewhat gradual, surface rooms were at first used for storage, while the pithouse continued to function as the residence. Later on, surface rooms were used for habitation. Pithouses were retained, however, with architectural details that suggest that their functions were no longer entirely domestic. By analogy to the semisubterranean rooms in modern Pueblo villages, these are called kivas by archaeologists.

In naming a prehistoric structure a kiva, the archaeologist is assuming a functional identity with a modern institution. This is a practice fraught with difficulty. For example, at most Pueblo villages today, kivas are used for rituals associated with the katchina ceremonies. However, it is not likely that the katchina belief system came into being much before 1250 or 1300. To refer to a pit structure built in A.D. 900 or 1000 as a kiva may be justified for a variety of reasons, but assumptions about what rituals, if any, were carried out in the structure must surely be suspect.

Similarly, when archaeologists assume that by A.D. 1000, pithouses had "become" kivas, it does not follow that thenceforward pithouses were never again used as ordinary residences. The archaeological record documents many "late pithouses." These are pithouses that appear to have been used exclusively for secular, residential purposes but were occupied at different times after A.D. 1000 when above-ground dwellings are the norm. The late pithouses are often clues to relatively short-term changes in settlement location and adjustments to climatic fluctuations. One interesting historic case that documents the use of pithouses as habitations comes from the founding of the Hopi village of Bacavi in the early part of this century. Bacavi was founded in 1909 after a factional dispute sundered the village of Oraibi. Those people who went to Bacavi arrived in the late fall, when there was no time to construct appropriate pueblo shelter before the cold of winter. So the first arrivals built pithouses in which to live during the winter months. Some of these were not only still standing, but were occupied in the 1970s.

As dwelling places, both pithouses and pueblo dwellings share thermal properties that are useful where the winters are very cold and there is little wood for fuel or building. In pithouses, the sunken floor of the dwelling below the frost line helps to moderate both winter and summer temperatures. The ground mass surrounding the sunken section of the house serves as a massive insulator. Similarly, the massed contiguous rooms of pueblos insulate the rooms from wind and cold. The thick adobe walls can act as Trombe walls, collecting solar heat during the day, and releasing it when temperatures drop at night. Further, neither pithouse or pueblo construction requires quantities of wood, or expensive building materials. Today, many non-Pueblo residents of the Southwest use these architectural principles and materials to construct thermally efficient dwellings. Yet, to assume that these properties were uppermost in the minds of the ancient builders is surely wrong, and it would be wildly speculative to try to guess what properties or values the ancient architects were following.

In the second half of the 20th century, the modern city of Santa Fe enacted a building code that dictates the style and vertical height of buildings for aesthetic reasons. Among other things, the code encourages the use of pueblo-style dwellings and earth colors for exterior walls. Today, entire neighborhoods of condominium housing in Santa Fe are virtually indistinguishable from

Acoma or Taos pueblos. The archaeologists of the future may be continuously puzzled, but it would clearly be a grave mistake for them to assume that Acoma and Taos pueblos and Santa Fe are functionally identical or were built in this way for the same reasons.

Today, as one drives into Pueblo villages, it is not uncommon to see some single family residences that are much like suburban residences anywhere in the United States. Behind these houses, however, there may be large adobe *hornos*, the bread ovens Pueblo women use for baking. Toward the center of the village, there will be open plazas, kept clear of vegetation. These may seem dusty and grim when deserted, but on a feast day, they are lined with colorfully clothed people who are watching wonderfully costumed Pueblos perform elaborate dances. At some dances, a shade at one end of the dance plaza may shelter the plaster image of a Catholic saint, in whose honor the traditional Native, non-Christian, dance is held.

Within the central part of the village, there will be houses with contiguous rooms, sometimes with two or more stories. In this part of the village, there will be one or more kivas that can be recognized by the wooden ladders protruding high above the entry hatches in the roofs. Sometimes a sign in English warns visitors away from the kivas. Surely visitors are lulled into feeling that they could have stepped back into the 13th century. Yet around the villages, to the rear or sides of houses, there are modern cars and farm equipment. Children play with the latest toys and wear the most up-to-date children's fashions. Depending on the village and the time of day, television sets may be on in most of the houses, as they would be anywhere. Much about the villages has changed. Yet living in the pueblos indicates a commitment to the traditional community and its values. No amount of television or number of John Deere tractors will turn the pueblo into a typical American suburb.

Continuity and change are readily appreciated in Pueblo pottery. The Pueblos have been making and using pottery for nearly 800 years, demonstrating their skill and versatility as potters by making very large storage vessels, jars in the shape of cylinders, symmetrical jars with flared shoulders, cooking and storage pots with intricately textured or smoothed and burnished surfaces, as well as painted bowls, jars, scoops, ladles, mugs, and canteens. Their craftsmanship and their art are reflected in their use of carbon- and mineral-based pigments, including lead glaze, and in painted designs that range from simple and elegant to intricately complicated. Pueblo pottery was produced without the wheel, yet is nonetheless thin and symmetrical. It was fired without a kiln, yet is nonetheless sturdy and well-fired. These characteristics continue in the work presently being made by Pueblo potters.

Today, Pueblo pottery is valued by art dealers and collectors throughout the world. Modern Pueblo pottery, as author Stephen Trimble reminds us, "is a tradition, but it is also a part of contemporary life. It is art—vital,

Traditional adobe dwellings in Taos Pueblo *(left)* are copied in these modern counterparts in Santa Fe *(right)*. Pueblo-style architecture, with its adobe walls and flat roofs supported by log vigas, is much admired in cities of the Southwest, where it is replicated in adobe or adobe-colored stucco. Taos Pueblo, like all pueblos, is a single community of people who are closely related and have known each other all their lives. The modern structures, by contrast, camouflage the single-family dwelling units of the 20th-century U.S.

everyday art—both a creation and a symbol for the Pueblo people." Nearly all of the pottery is made using only traditional technology. Clays, slip clay, and pigments are quarried and prepared, not purchased. Vessels are still formed and painted by hand and fired out in the open air. Pueblo potters today are both serious artists and traditional artisans. For example, clay is quarried from specific, established, sometimes secret, sources and is not taken out of the earth without ritual and prayer. The potter cleans, mixes, cures, and cares for the clay, and must be at peace with the world while forming the compositions. Making pottery is very serious work that results in something pleasing.

Over the centuries, the designs and styles of Pueblo pottery have varied regionally and over time. Some styles seem to have been simply the result of using customary decoration, learned by observing other potters. These were made in restricted areas and persisted with only slight modifications over time. Good examples are types such as Jemez, Taos, or Black Mesa Black-on-white. Other styles occur on pottery over very large areas sometimes for relatively short periods of time. Pinedale style is a good example. In some cases, elements and motifs go together, carrying suggested meaning. Pinedale style is a good example here, too. The elements include the parrots, snakes, and horned serpents that are inferentially related to water control and fertility in the iconography of the suggested Southwestern Cult.

Among today's Pueblo potters each village also has a distinctive style. Modern elements and motifs are identical to those used centuries ago. Yet, the context in which the modern styles developed and the functions they now serve are very different from those of the past. From the 1880s, when the intercontinental railroad was put through in the Southwest, the stations provided an opportunity for travelers to see, and to buy, Native American crafts. All of the Pueblos were terribly poor, and the few pennies they earned selling pottery to tourists helped, although inadequately. In the early 1900s, an interesting and fortunate combination of institutions and people began what would later be called the Pueblo pottery revival.

The Southwest, particularly Santa Fe and Taos, became a haven for artists and writers who developed a genuine interest in Native Americans. At the same time, archaeologists, backed by East Coast money, began excavation projects, established research institutions and museums, and frequently hired Pueblo labor. Just such fortuitous circumstances were the stimulus for the work of Maria and Julian Martinez of San Ildefonso Pueblo and Nampeyo and Lesou of Hano. Edgar Lee Hewett, as director of the new School of American Research, began working on the Pajarito Plateau at what is now Bandelier National Monument in 1907. Among the men he hired to work was Julian Martinez. Maria, then 20 and an experienced potter, was with her husband at the field camp and became very interested in the pottery being excavated. Hewett asked her if she could reproduce the pottery. After thoughtful study, Maria and Julian Martinez made pieces that were not simply reproductions, but objects of art in themselves. Greatly pleased with the results, Hewett purchased the pieces and encouraged future work much of which he brought to Santa Fe for sale. Later, with additional reassurance from Kenneth Chapman and others, the Martinez husband-and-wife team sold their work directly to the public at the Museum of New Mexico.

The first pottery the couple made and sold was polychrome, similar to the archaeological pieces Hewett had excavated. By 1915, Maria Martinez and other San Ildefonso potters were able to sell the polished black ware they had long been producing, but Maria Martinez's work was technically superior—larger and better polished—to the others. In 1919, the Martinezes began experiments that allowed them to successfully produce the black-on-black ware for which they became world famous.

It was Julian Martinez who painted the designs on the pottery—always. He loved the painting and kept notebooks with sketches he had made from sherds from archaeological sites and work he saw in museums. Of his hallmark designs, the *awanyu* or plumed serpent, with a lightning tongue, appeared on the polychrome pottery of the Pajarito Plateau and the radiating feather motif on Mimbres pottery brought to the museum in Santa Fe.

The story of Nampeyo and Lesou is similar. Lesou found work in the 1890s with the archaeological crews then excavating Sikyatki Ruin under Jesse W. Fewkes. Thomas Keam, who began his trading post in 1875, commissioned replicas of some of the Sikyatki polychrome pots in part because of his great

Maria and Julian Martinez, of San Ildefonso Pueblo, spearheaded the revival of Pueblo pottery among the Rio Grande pueblos. Maria Martinez formed and polished the vessels that her husband then painted. Seen below is an example of their work, produced in the mid-1930s, and decorated with an *awanyu*, or plumed serpent.

interest in Hopi culture and also to sell as tourist items. By 1900, Nampeyo had revived the Sikyatki style, and through it developed her own, individual, interpretive treatment and art. Keam was able to ensure a market for her work. The Sikyatki revival style is a yellow ware. It thus reverts to the colors and motifs used at Hopi before the 1700s when Hopi returned from their sojourn at Zuni, Acoma, Zia, and elsewhere, bringing with them the black-on-white pottery that they then produced. The revival style also uses motifs derived from the sacred realm. While these are sold to tourists, the designs on some of them are considered holy. For instance, the feathers painted on pottery are prayers in the way that prayer plumes are prayers.

Today, Pueblo potters are artists. The traders and purveyors of this art have encouraged each village to develop its own style that would be recognized, and sought after, by collectors. Yet through the inspiration from the ancient pottery closest at hand, each village, each artist reconnected to the traditions of the past. Symbols were reinvented, reinterpreted, and recaptured. In the art of Nampeyo's great-great-granddaughter Hisi (Camille) Nampeyo and Maria Martinez's great-granddaughter Wan Povi (Kathy Sanchez), who today are young women, the symbols have been passed on to new generations of potters.

What are some of the other legacies the ancient Pueblo have bequeathed the world? Pueblo peoples did not domesticate corn. That occurred far to the south in tropical Mexico. But the Pueblo ancestors did develop and cul-

tivate varieties of maize adapted to the spring drought and short dry growing seasons of the Southwest. Pueblo agricultural practices consistently
maintained genetic diversity in seed stock; variation itself was valued.
Furthermore, the Pueblo agricultural technology, the knowledge of where,
when, and how to plant includes information important to the success of
Pueblo peoples as farmers. The key to Pueblo agriculture is the maintenance
of heterogeneity, a strategy that is diametrically opposite to that pursued
today in modern agribusiness.

Maize is the third most economically important grain in the world, after
wheat and rice. It is grown on every continent but Antarctica, often in soils
that are not appropriate for either wheat or rice. In our over-populated world
where desertification continues and few can afford high-tech solutions to
environmental degradation, where millions go hungry and droughts take a
devastating toll in human life, Pueblo maize and agricultural knowledge may
truly make a difference. It can provide new seed stock and methods of planting that make it possible for more people to survive and to contribute to the
future of humankind.

Another part of the Pueblo legacy, perhaps, is providing an alternative
perspective to the European-American value system. Such is clearly the case
for historian Will Roscoe, whose book, *The Zuni Man-Woman*, on the life
of We'-Wha, the most famous of the Zuni *berdaches*, climbed to the national bestseller charts in 1991. (Many Native American tribes contained
berdaches—individuals who assumed some of the gender roles of the opposite sex. They were not only accepted, but were highly regarded.) Roscoe
writes that the Western category of homosexuality is an historical construct.
He suggests that as a society, we would benefit from using examples, such as
the berdaches of other cultures, to improve our own understanding and to
free our categorizations of their cultural bias.

Roscoe is too perceptive and intelligent to either portray modern Zuni as
unchanged, or to advocate the adoption of Zuni values outside their historical
and cultural contexts. Rather, he calls for developing a multidimensional paradigm for understanding the usefulness of diversity when creating attitudes and
behaviors regarding gender roles.

There is an additional aspect of Pueblo philosophy that would prove useful in other cultural contexts. This is the Pueblo ability to incorporate change
in order to remain the same. It is a process by which a people, secure in their
values, accept innovation that is appropriate and that allows their basic system of values to remain intact. Were this process a skill that could be transferred and learned in other settings, perhaps there would be less violence
when fundamentalism—of any sort—encounters the diverse beliefs and ethical systems of the world. The Pueblo lessons, time and again, are lessons in
the value of diversity. And to maintain diversity, it is necessary to guard
ancient wisdoms for the future.

REFERENCES

The literature of southwestern archaeology and of Pueblo ethnography is vast. My own small working library has about 2000 volumes. University libraries have many times that number of books on these subjects. In addition to books and serial publications, much of the important literature is published in professional journals and in publications of U.S. government agencies. Finally, there is an important "gray literature" that consists of reports printed in limited quantities by federal and state agencies and by private archaeological consulting firms, as part of the legal procedures for demonstrating compliance with antiquities and cultural heritage legislation. Rather than attempt to select materials from all of these sources, I have limited the references provided here to a few, generally available books and articles that are also accessible to interested readers who may not possess the technical vocabulary of Southwest archaeology. I believe these sources will reward efforts to read them.

CHAPTER I

CORDELL, LINDA S. 1984 *Prehistory of the Southwest*. Academic Press, Inc., Orlando, San Diego, New York.

DOZIER, EDWARD P. 1970 The Pueblo Indians of North America. Holt, Rinehart and Winston, Inc., New York.

JONES, DEWITT AND LINDA S. CORDELL 1985 *Anasazi World*. Graphic Arts Center, Portland.

KESSEL, JOHN L. 1989 Spaniards and Pueblos: from crusading intolerance to pragmatic accommodation, pp. 127-138 in *Columbian Consequences, Volume 1, Archaeological and Historical Perspectives on the Spanish Borderlands West*, edited by David Hurst Thomas. Smithsonian Institution Press, Washington and London.

LOMAWAIMA, HARTMAN, H. 1989 Hopification, a strategy for cultural preservation, pp. 93-99 in *Columbian Consequences, Volume 1, Archaeological and Historical Perspectives on the Spanish Borderlands West*, edited by David Hurst Thomas. Smithsonian Institution Press, Washington and London.

SANDO, JOE S. 1992 *Pueblo Nations Eight Centuries of Pueblo Indian History*. Clear Light Publishers, Santa Fe.

CHAPTER 2

AMSDEN, CHARLES AVERY 1949 *Prehistoric Southwesterners from Basketmaker to Pueblo*. Southwest Museum, Los Angeles.

FRISON, GEORGE C. AND BRUCE A. BRADLEY 1980 *Folsom Tools and Technology at the Hanson Site, Wyoming*. University of New Mexico Press, Albuquerque.

GREENBERG, JOSEPH H., CHRISTY G. TURNER II, AND STEPHEN L. ZEGURA 1986 The Settlement of the Americas: a Comparison of the Linguistic, Dental, and Genetic Evidence, *Current Anthropology* 27(5): 477-97.

MACNEISH, RICHARD S. 1993 *The 1992 Excavations of Pendejo and Pintada Caves Near Orogrande, New Mexico, An AFAR and Fort Bliss Archaeological Project*. Andover Foundation for Archaeological Research, Andover, MA.

MELTZER, DAVID J. 1993 *Search for the First Americans*. St. Remy Press, Montréal; Smithsonian Books, Washington.

STANFORD, DENNIS J. AND JANE S. DAY (EDITORS) 1992 *Ice Age Hunters of the Rockies*. Denver Museum of Natural History and University Press of Colorado.

CHAPTER 3

FOSTER, NELSON AND LINDA S. CORDELL (EDITORS) 1992 *Chilies to Chocolate: Food the Americas Gave the World*. University of Arizona Press, Tucson.

MATSON, R.G. 1991 *The Origins of Southwestern Agriculture*. The University of Arizona Press, Tucson and London.

NABHAN, GARY PAUL 1989 *Enduring Seeds, Native American Agriculture and Wild Plant Conservation*. North Point Press, San Francisco.

WEATHERFORD, JACK M. 1988 *Indian Givers. How the Indians of the Americas Transformed the World*. Fawcett Columbine, New York.

WILLS, WIRT H. 1988 *Early Prehistoric Agriculture in the American Southwest*. School of American Research Press, Santa Fe.

CHAPTER 4

BRODY, J.J. 1977 *Mimbres Painted Pottery*. School of American Research, Santa Fe.

BRODY, J.J., CATHERINE J. SCOTT AND STEVEN A. LEBLANC 1983 *Mimbres Pottery, Ancient Art of the American Southwest*. Hudson Hills Press, New York.

GILMAN, PATRICIA A. 1987 Architecture as Artifact: Pitstructures and Pueblos in the American Southwest, *American Antiquity*, 53(3): 538-564.

HAURY, EMIL W. 1936 The Mogollon Culture of Southwestern New Mexico, *Medallion Papers 20*, Gila Pueblo, Globe, Arizona.

LEBLANC, STEVEN A. 1989 Cultural Dynamics in the Southern Mogollon Area, pp. 179-207 in *Dynamics of Southwest Prehistory*, edited by Linda S. Cordell and George J. Gumerman, Smithsonian Institution Press, Washington.

REID, J. JEFFERSON 1989 A Grasshopper Perspective on the Mogollon of the Arizona Mountains, pp. 65-97 in *Dynamics of Southwest Prehistory*, edited by Linda S. Cordell and George J. Gumerman, Smithsonian Institution Press, Washington.

SHAFER, HARRY J. AND ANNA J. TAYLOR 1986 Mimbres Mogollon Pueblo Dynamics and Ceramic Style Change. *Journal of Field Archaeology* 13(1): 43-68.

CHAPTER 5

MCNITT, FRANK K. 1957 *Richard Wetherill: Anasazi, Pioneer Explorer of Southwestern Ruins.* Revised Edition, University of New Mexico Press, Albuquerque.

CORDELL, LINDA S. 1984 *Prehistory of the Southwest* pp. 49-119. Academic Press, Inc., Orlando, San Diego, New York.

GUMERMAN, GEORGE J. AND JEFFREY S. DEAN 1989 Prehistoric Cooperation and Competition in the Western Anasazi Area, pp. 99-148 in *Dynamics of Southwest Prehistory*, edited by Linda S. Cordell and George J. Gumerman, Smithsonian Institution Press, Washington.

REED, LORI STEPHENS AND PAUL F. REED, (EDITORS) 1992 *Cultural Diversity and Adaptation: The Archaic, Anasazi, and Navajo Occupation of the Upper San Juan Basin,* New Mexico Bureau of Land Management Cultural Resources Series No. 9, Farmington.

CHAPTER 6

GABRIEL, KATHRYN 1991 *Roads to Center Place, A Cultural Atlas of Chaco Canyon and the Anasazi.* Johnson Books, Boulder.

JUDGE, W. JAMES 1989 Chaco Canyon—San Juan Basin, pp. 209-261 in *Dynamics of Southwest Prehistory*, edited by Linda S. Cordell and George J. Gumerman, Smithsonian Institution Press, Washington.

LEKSON, STEPHEN H. 1984 *Great Pueblo Architecture of Chaco Canyon, New Mexico.* Publications in Archaeology 18B, Chaco Canyon Studies, National Park Service, USDI, Albuquerque.

SEBASTIAN, LYNNE 1992 *The Chaco Anasazi: Sociopolitical evolution in the prehistoric Southwest.* Cambridge University Press, Cambridge.

VIVIAN, R. GWINN 1990 *The Chacoan Prehistory of the San Juan Basin.* Academic Press, Inc., San Diego, New York, Boston.

CHAPTER 7

BRADLEY, BRUCE A. 1992 Excavations at Sand Canyon Pueblo, pp. 79-99 in *The Sand Canyon Archaeological Project, A Progress Report*, edited by William D. Lipe, Crow Canyon Archaeological Center, Cortez, Colorado.

CORDELL, LINDA S. 1985 Why did they leave and where did they go?, pp. 35-39 in *Exploration.* School of American Research, Santa Fe.

DEAN, JEFFREY S. 1986 Tsé Yaa Kin: Houses Beneath the Rock, pp. 2-13 in *Houses Beneath the Rock, Canyon de Chelly, Navajo National Monument.* in *Exploration.* School of American Research, Santa Fe.

FOWLER, ANDREW AND JOHN R. STEIN 1992 The Anasazi Great House in Space, Time, and Paradigm, pp. 101-122 in *Anasazi Regional Organization and the Chaco System*, edited by David E. Doyel. *Maxwell Museum of Anthropology, Anthropological Papers* No. 5, Albuquerque.

MORRIS, DON P. 1986 National Park Service, USDI, Washington.

ROHN, ARTHUR H. 1971 *Mug House, Mesa Verde National Park—Colorado.* National Park Service Archeological Research Series—7D, Washington.

CHAPTER 8

ADAMS, E. CHARLES 1991 *The Origin and Development of the Pueblo Katsina Cult.* University of Arizona Press, Tucson.

CROWN, PATRICIA L. 1994 *Ceramics and Ideology, Salado Polychromes Pottery.* University of New Mexico Press, Albuquerque.

DI PESO, CHARLES C. 1974 *Casas Grandes: A Fallen Trading Center of the Gran Chichimeca.* Amerind Foundation Publication, No. 9, Dragoon, Arizona.

REED, LORI STEPHENS AND PAUL F. REED, (EDITORS) 1992 *Cultural Diversity and Adaptation: The Archaic, Anasazi, and Navajo Occupation of the Upper San Juan Basin,* New Mexico Bureau of Land Management Cultural Resource Series No. 9, Farmington, NM.

RILEY, CARROLL L. 1987 *The Frontier People, The Greater Southwest in the Protohistoric Period.* Revised and Expanded Edition, University of New Mexico Press, Albuquerque.

UPHAM, STEADMAN 1982 *Politics and Power: An Economic and Political History of the Western Pueblo.* Academic Press, New York.

CHAPTER 9

ADAMS, E. CHARLES 1982 *Walpi Archaeological Project: Synthesis and Interpretation.* Museum of Northern Arizona, Flagstaff.

ANONYMOUS 1987 *When Cultures Meet Remembering San Gabriel del Yunge Oweenge*, Papers from the October 20, 1984 Conference held at San Juan Pueblo, New Mexico. Sunstone Press, Sante Fe.

KESSELL, JOHN L. 1979 *Kiva, Cross and Crown, The Pecos Indians and New Mexico 1540-1840.* National Park Service, USDI, Washington.

LOMAWAIMA, HARTMAN H. 1989 Hopification, a Strategy for Cultural Preservation, pp. 93-99 in *Columbian Consequences, Volume 1*, Archaeological and Historical Perspectives on the Spanish Borderlands West, edited by David Hurst Thomas. Smithsonian Institution Press, Washington and London.

MONTGOMERY, ROSS G., WATSON SMITH, AND JOHN OTIS BREW 1949 *Franciscan Awatovi: The Excavation and Conjectural Reconstruction of a 17th-Century Spanish Mission Establishment at a Hopi Indian Town in Northeastern Arizona.* Papers of the Peabody Museum of American Archaeology. Harvard University, vol. 36. Cambridge.

SPIVEY, RICHARD L. 1979 *Maria.* Revised and Expanded Edition. Northland Press, Flagstaff.

SPIELMANN, KATHERINE A. (EDITOR) 1991 *Farmers, Hunters, and Colonists Interaction Between the Southwest and the Southern Plains.* The University of Arizona Press, Tucson.

TRIMBLE, STEPHEN 1987 *Talking with the Clay. The Art of Pueblo Pottery.* School of American Research Press, Santa Fe.

INDEX

PICTURE CREDITS

Front cover photograph by George H. H. Huey
Back cover photograph by David Muench

AUTHOR'S ACKNOWLEDGMENTS

The opportunity to write this book came to me during a time of personal and professional transition. As I packed yet another box of books and crate of dishes, I suspected that accepting the challenge this book offered—at the time it came along—was probably slightly crazy. Yet doing the book allowed me to rethink, and then to share, the archaeology of a region and its people, my intellectual and emotional anchor for 25 years. There is more than enough to sustain me for another 25 years.

Archaeology in the Pueblo Southwest has developed tremendously over the last few decades. The creative intelligence and enthusiasm of a younger generation of archaeologists assures that it will continue to grow and provide insights into and appreciation for Pueblo people and their ancestors. Not all the new information has come from the very young. I am thankful to the ever-young archaeologists, (Richard) "Scotty" MacNeish, John Ware, and Edmund Ladd for inviting me to visit their excavations and laboratories to discuss the latest finds. There is also a new excitement as Native Pueblo scholars and traditional leaders share their interests and concerns about how their past is written. As novel information becomes available and new interpretations—reflecting different systems of value—are written, ongoing learning is assured. I thank all of those who continue to contribute to this body of knowledge.

I am grateful to my valued colleague, and series editor, Jeremy Sabloff, for giving me the chance to write this book. He and the staff at St. Remy Press, particularly Carolyn Jackson, Philippe Arnoldi, Alfred LeMaitre, and Jenny Meltzer, and Patricia Gallagher at Smithsonian Books were consistently patient and helpful throughout the process of producing this book.

My friends Hartman and Tsianina Lomawaima, Desha Robin Hill, and Vincent Yannie read all or parts of the manuscript, offered excellent advice and their own invaluable perspectives. It is a pleasure to say thank you.

Linda S. Cordell
Boulder, Colorado